CHRISTIAN PRESENCE SERIES

EDITOR: M. A. C. WARREN

❖

Sandals at the Mosque

lifetime's travel and study in the Islamic world, and from many intimate friendships, Dr. Cragg seeks to show Christians the Christian meaning of the depths of Muslim religious thought and experience, and how in that setting to preach the Gospel in the humility which befits those who would proclaim One who humbled himself to the death of the cross.

The book requires no previous knowledge of Islam or of 'comparative religion.' A helpful glossary of Arabic religious terms and a book-list for further study are included.

DR. KENNETH CRAGG is an Anglican clergyman, co-editor of *The Muslim World,* and a leading Christian student of Islam. He was for several years Adjunct Professor of Philosophy at the American University of Beirut in Lebanon and from 1951 to 1956 was Professor of Arabic and Islamics at the Hartford Seminary Foundation in Connecticut. Since then he has been on a special assignment with the Study Program in Islamics of the Near East Christian Council, in which he has lectured throughout the various Muslim lands of the Middle East to both Christian and Muslim groups. The Study Program has its headquarters in Jerusalem, where Dr. Cragg is Canon of St. George's Cathedral. He is now resident in Canterbury, England, as a Fellow of St. Augustine's College with continuing responsibilities in Jerusalem. He is also author of the well-known *The Call of the Minaret* and translator of *City of Wrong.*

KENNETH CRAGG

Sandals at the Mosque

>>> ❖ <<<

Christian Presence Amid

ISLAM

Oxford University Press

New York

1959

Muhammedism — relations — Christianity
Christianity and other religions — muhammedism

PRINTED IN GREAT BRITAIN

General Introduction

>>> ✧ <<<

CHRISTIANS are being presented by the contemporary world with what is, in many ways, a unique opportunity of demonstrating the Gospel. Scarcely less unique is the opportunity being offered to them of discovering in a new and deeper way what that Gospel is. Those are large claims. Can they be justified?

What is this unique opportunity? At the very least it is the opportunity presented to Christians to demonstrate the fundamental truth of the Gospel that it is a universal message, whose relevance is not limited to any one culture, to any one system of thought, to any one pattern of activity. That is by no means the truism that it may appear to be. For more than four centuries the expansion of the Christian Church has coincided with the economic, political and cultural expansion of Western Europe. Viewed from the standpoint of the peoples of Asia, and to a growing extent from that of the peoples of Africa, this expansion has been an aggressive attack on their own way of life. Quite inevitably the Christian faith has for many in these lands been inextricably bound up with this Western aggression. But it has also to be admitted quite frankly that during these centuries the missionaries of the Christian Church have commonly assumed that Western civilization and Christianity were two aspects of the same gift which they were commissioned to offer to the rest of mankind.

5

This assumption was sometimes quite conscious and was explicitly stated. More often it was quite unconscious and would have been indignantly denied. But in neither case are we called upon to judge our fathers. Their sincerity can hardly be disputed. Their self-sacrificing devotion finds its monument today in the world-wide diffusion of the Christian faith, the existence, in almost every country of the world, of a community of Christians recognizably part of the Universal Church.

What we are called upon to recognize is that in the world of our time there is a widespread revolt against any form of domination by the West. Nations whose political independence was only achieved 'yesterday' or is only about to be achieved 'tomorrow' can be excused for having their own interpretation of the past, an interpretation unlikely to coincide with that which is prevalent in the West. This very waning of Western influence is in part our Christian opportunity. We are freer today than we have ever been to serve the Gospel without the risk of confusion between that Gospel and the 'power' of the West.

But that is not all. The peoples of Asia and Africa, in their revolt against domination by the West, are presenting a specific challenge to the Christian faith. In what does this consist?

There are three main ingredients in this challenge.

First there is a critical evaluation of the Christian religion which rejects it as something inherently Western, as something which fails to correspond to the *felt* needs of Asia and Africa. Christianity is, in such judgment, altogether too Western in its character and in the form which it assumes in its local manifestations. This rejection is the more serious in that Asian and African peoples are themselves, like us in the West, confronted by the bewildering demands of the modern world. All the old landmarks are disappearing. Everywhere there is a desperate search for some inner basis of security, some inner assurance which can enable men and women to face the storm. In the sequel, particularly in Asia, but not only there, the peoples of these countries are seeking to find this psychic security by digging deep into their own past. This is at once an expression of their revolt against the West and one explanation of the renaissance of the great ethnic religions. Further to this it is to be noted that in a new way these ancient religions are becoming themselves missionary. No longer content to be on the defensive, they are offering themselves as answers to the questionings of mankind.

Here is a situation which is new. Only once before, and then in its earliest centuries, has the Christian Church had to face a comparable challenge to its claim to meet the deepest needs of man's heart and mind. The devotees of Mithras, the mystery cults of the Mediterranean world, the Gnostics in that earlier day were serious competitors with the message of the Gospel. Their appeal failed. There followed the long thousand years during which Europe was isolated from the rest of mankind and built for itself its own peculiar civilization. Then suddenly, drawing on its inner dynamism, a dynamism closely related to its faith, the European world overflowed its narrow boundaries and began its great expansion. For a time it appeared as if nothing could arrest this expansion. It is of some importance to recognize that it is by no means certain that anything can! The scientific view of the world, with all its implications about human survival, is Western in origin. Communism and nationalism are Western concepts. It may well be doubted if anything can arrest the advance of all mankind towards something like a common civilization – if common destruction is avoided. Nevertheless there is, at the moment, a significant pause in the impetus of Western expansion in its Christian expression. The challenge to Christians is precisely this that the ethnic religions as well as secularist philosophies of life are offering themselves as the basis of the new world civilization. Both deny the relevance of Christianity.

The *second* challenge follows from the first. Can the Christian faith not only prove its ability to meet the deep human needs of our time but also make peoples of different cultural backgrounds feel at home in the new world? This is a more complex task than would appear. For it is part of our paradoxical situation that, at a moment when the world is becoming so obviously interdependent, every nation in it is seeking to assert its own independence. And religion and culture are the means by which independence is asserted. Has the Christian Church got a Gospel to meet this situation? We may put the question this way – can the Christians of the West accept the fact that the expression which Christianity will receive in its Asian and African forms may well be, almost certainly will be, in many respects very different indeed from what we know in the West? That again could be worded as follows – are we of the West prepared to trust the Holy Spirit to lead the Christians of Asia and Africa, or must a controlling Western hand be permanently resting on the Ark of God? Let no one imagine that those questions will find an easy or unanimous response from Western Christians.

There remains a *third* challenge. The Christian Church has not yet seriously faced the theological problem of 'co-existence' with other religions. The very term seems to imply the acceptance of some limitation of the universal relevance of the Gospel. Can that be accepted? It can hardly be doubted that the answer must be 'no'. Are we then shut up to the alternative of what in some disguise or other must be an aggressive attack on the deeply held convictions of those who live by other faiths than our own?

This projected series of volumes has been designed to express a deliberate recognition of the challenge outlined above and to suggest that there is a way in which they can be met without any betrayal of the Gospel – indeed in deeper loyalty to that Gospel's real content.

First of the demands presented to us by this understanding of the contemporary world is a *glad* acceptance of the new situation in which the Christian faith can everywhere be distinguished from its past historical association with Western political, economic and cultural aggression. Here is the 'great new fact of our time', every whit as great a fact as the existence of the Church in every land. Here is our great new opportunity, even though it may well be an opportunity to witness through suffering. The Cross, after all, was not a symbol of imperial domination but of the *imperium* of sacrifice. The Christian faith has nothing to lose by suffering. In and through suffering it can perhaps speak home to the hearts and minds of suffering mankind better than in any other way.

Second of the demands upon us, to march with our gladness, is a deep humility, by which we remember that God has not left Himself without witness in any nation at any time. When we approach the man of another faith than our own it will be in a spirit of expectancy to find how God has been speaking to him and what new understandings of the grace and love of God we may ourselves discover in this encounter.

Our first task in approaching another people, another culture, another religion, is to take off our shoes, for the place we are approaching is holy. Else we may find ourselves treading on men's dreams. More serious still, we may forget that God was here before our arrival. We have, then, to ask what is the authentic religious content in the experience of the Muslim, the Hindu, the Buddhist, or whoever he may be. We may, if we have asked humbly and respectfully, still reach the conclusion that our brothers have started from a false premise and reached a faulty conclusion. But we must not arrive at our judgment from outside their religious situation. We have to try to sit where they sit, to enter sympathetically into the pains and griefs and joys of their history and see how those pains and griefs and joys have determined the premises of their argument. We have, in a word, to be 'present' with them.

This is what is meant by the title of this series – *The Christian Presence* amid Islam, Hinduism, Buddhism. . . . This will not be an easy approach. But then the love of God is not easy.

The first volume in this series treats of the Christian Presence amid Islam. The author, Dr Kenneth Cragg, starts from the conviction, born of his own experience in the world of Islam, that Christianity itself is vitally concerned with the same underlying themes that are at the heart of Islam. That is a very important starting point. It begins with what Christians have in common with Muslims. Here is an attitude of mind which is meant to govern all our relations with our fellow-men. It is what St Paul was writing about in Romans, chapters 2 and 3. This is a fundamental insight of the Gospel which is sometimes overlooked by those engaged in the Christian Mission.

So Dr Cragg introduces us first of all to a gathering of Muslims when they are worshipping together in a mosque. From here he takes us on into that world of 'meeting' in which we all find ourselves whether we like it or not. Being 'present' in this way we are able to see the relevance of our

Gospel and to pray that others may recognize it also. This is 'frontier' theology, a theology born of the experiences we have when we move out from our own central assumptions to meet the central assumptions of other men. Writing elsewhere of this experience of the 'frontier' Dr Cragg says:

. . . it would be folly for the Christian Church to neglect the deeper reaches of the Islamic heritage on the plea that the average Muslim is himself unaware of them. Nor need there be any fear that by seeking the fullest patterns of relationship the Church would . . . 'be making Muslims more self-consciously Muslim and so more resistant to Christianity'. 'With what measure ye mete it shall be measured to you again' remains the spiritual principle of all Christian trusteeship of truth. If we would in the end bespeak an adequate Muslim awareness of Christ we must essay an adequate Christian awareness of Islam. . . .

In another place Dr Cragg has also written:

There is . . . a great need for a discerning Christian trusteeship of Christ which can undertake an irenic and yet loyal witness to the meaning of the Gospel, without capitulating either to easy neglect of truth or to assertive and alienating advocacy of it.

In quoting that last paragraph I have also indicated the spirit in which this series has been undertaken and in which it is hoped that this and subsequent volumes will be read.

M. A. C. WARREN

His vocation was one of being present among people
with a presence willed and intended as a witness to
the love of Christ.

(of Charles de Foucauld)

Table of Contents

Part 1

IN QUEST OF ISLAM

Part 2

CONDITIONS OF INTER-RELIGION

Part 3
PRESENT WITH THE PEACE OF GOD

Table of Contents

To
KAMEL HUSSEIN
and
DAUD RAHBAR
in grateful greeting

Foreword

>>> ✧ <<<

THE father of a pupil of William Blake, the poet-engraver, was, it is recorded, Muster-Master-General of the British Army in the years of the Napoleonic War. The business of his picturesque office was to oversee the work of lesser Muster-Masters who were officers specially charged with the reviewing of regiments. They had to vouch that the names on the pay-roll represented the actual regimental strength, this being a necessary precaution in days when commanders were tempted to swell the ranks with fictitious names.

It is not known that there was ever any effective spiritual counterpart of such an office. The faiths of the world have their characteristic points of muster in temple, mosque or church. But no census of religious allegiance can be taken by merely external means. The problem of integrity of adherence and confession abides in every situation and fictions of belonging inevitably creep into the roll-call of belief and devotion. The underlying idea of this book is that the human situation itself, as it has come to be in this bewildering and exacting time, acts as a searching Muster-Master-General of the worlds of faith. Man reaches ever farther outwards into space and so doing deepens the issues that belong in the inward spaces of the heart. Men with their faiths have more mystery and urgency in common than at any earlier point in history. They are, so to speak, at muster to answer for

B

what is in them: their ranks are the religions and the cultures out of which they respond.

Within this thought, attention is concentrated upon the two faiths of Islam and Christianity. Since sandals are a familiar sight at the mosque when Muslims gather and since they have also a significant place in a well-known New Testament passage that has to do with devotion under test, they are taken as a symbol of our whole theme. Leaving their sandals at the threshold of the mosque, Muslims present themselves for the congregational expression of their loyalty vouching, as it were, for the validity of their belonging in the terms of the minaret's summons. When they retake their sandals, it is to go out into the day to day world which is the arena of the things they mean.

It may seem an idle fancy to build a theme so imponderable as Muslim-Christian meeting around a token so slight. And truly, stacks of shoes in neat boxes on a vendor's shelves do little to excite the imagination. It is surely different with the assorted footwear which accumulates outside the mosque, worn and torn in the ways of life and dusty with the actual world. In Robinson Crusoe's epic you may remember, 'two shoes that were not fellows' suffice to bring a most graphic sense of desolating shipwreck as they lay ownerless upon the beach. There is eloquence, too, in the new shoes that were part of the welcome of the footsore prodigal when he returned to his father's house – even though it be right to surmise that his longest journey was ended. Perhaps, then, the miscellaneous sandals at the mosque can serve us for a title and a token.

To weave a study round them at the rendezvous of Muslim worship and to ponder the world around the rendezvous is the business of Part 1: 'In Quest of Islam'. What, we ask, are the thoughts of the man in the Muslim shoes? How does the muster find him, as it is reviewed by his own conscience and exhorted by the learned officers of his community of belief and law?

In what capacity, however, can outsiders present themselves on such occasions? Only on the plea of the larger context already noted, only as aware of the wider setting of time's whole relation to eternity and of the common world of human misery and grandeur. To explore this plea, Part 2 considers the 'Conditions of Inter-Religion', arguing that, whatever the sandals, men are more and more walking in a world of like predicament and mutual involvement. We may be outsiders to each other's systems of authority and devotion, but none are outsiders to humanity and the God with whom we have to do. The title of this part is deliberately chosen, but because of the objections to which it may be open, is carefully examined.

Responding to his name in this world, what does the Christian have to say of his allegiance and his loyalty? Part 3: 'Present with the Peace of God' attempts an answer. The phrase is from the familiar description in the Epistle to the Ephesians which seems to have come from a Roman parade ground. 'The shoes of the relevance of the Gospel of peace' are interpreted to illustrate one single, but central, area of Christian meaning and its communication to Islam. This is intended to exemplify the sort of duties in truth and love which the Christian Church has in relation to the faith and practice of Muslim fellow-men in this twentieth century, wherever Muslim society wrestles in personal and general terms with being Islamic.

So this book is in no sense an exposition of Islam. Nor is it a history of doctrines and institutions. It is not a manual of Islamics. Many such exist. The writer, for his part, has elsewhere tried to set forth some kindred topics which would otherwise have had to find a place. This is a reasonable explanation of their omission here. Slighter than *The Call of the Minaret* and pre-supposing its arguments, this venture is intended as a sequel and has a somewhat different aim. It has partly in mind certain critics of the earlier book, who insisted that while its substance might be sound, its intention was pointless. Religions, they asserted, must be content to keep apart, at least in their theological heart. 'Frontier theology' they regard as a waste of time. It is useless, they allege, to try to interpret what one of them calls 'the whole soteriology of Christianity' to Muslim thought or ethos, since these can never be expected to approve.

The pages that follow are impenitently contrary to this despair about Muslim-Christian mutuality, this isolationism of the Spirit. Christian faith, though traditionally, in many of its central items, inadmissible for Muslims, is vitally concerned with the same underlying themes that are at the heart of Islam. One crucial area of this inter-involvement is examined in Part 3 where the vast corollaries of the Islamic rejection of idols and the Islamic affirmation of God's unity are seen to be, not only in themselves deeply Christian things, but emphatically to involve the whole Christian meaning of redemptive love. For it is only in these terms that the last idols are dethroned and men liberated into the love of God. 'The God to end gods', 'the revelation to end revelation' – these are the inclusive common convictions of Islam and Christianity. The immense differences within them lie at the heart of reality and at the centre of the meaning of life. Whether or not we draw them together in spiritual meeting, they belong together in spiritual truth.

Nor do the times allow us to live in splendid isolation with no expressive reach of relevance. With acknowledgments to John Wesley, we must insist that the world has less and less

Foreword

room for a solitary Christian. It should, therefore, have less and less room for a secluded theology. Rightly we have our areas of theological discipline – Biblical theology, systematic theology, pastoral theology, ascetic theology and the like, in order to study our documentary sources, our total dogmas, our communal and personal patterns of life in belief. But for all their undoubted validity, they are inward and in the right sense 'ecclesiastical'. They have to do with the community, the *ecclesia* of faith. Why not also a theology that is outward and relational, having to do not merely with what is for those within but what offers for those without – a theology, in short, which is on the frontiers of religions in their mutual existence?

Such a theology in fact has the oldest and surest of Christian precedents. It is the central intellectual and spiritual activity of the New Testament itself. Here we are concerned to ponder only its broadest outlines in special relation to Islam, and, so doing, 'never to let ourselves close up inside out of a faint heart or a weary mind'.[1]

KENNETH CRAGG

Jerusalem,
Jordan

[1] R. Voillaume, *Seeds of the Desert*, Burns, Oates, London, 1955, p. 180. The quotation is changed here from 'yourselves' to 'ourselves'.

PART 1

In Quest of Islam

>>> ✧ <<<

IN AT THE GATE

'You have come to see our country from afar'. It was true enough. E. G. Browne, who records the conversation in his *A Year among the Persians*, had journeyed to Shiraz and Isfahan from the remoteness of Cambridge, England – a far country indeed for his Persian interlocuter. He had travelled by means more strenuous and devious than fall to the lot of the contemporary, and mostly airborne, orientalist. It was, then, with proper feeling that the Persian continued: 'Do not, like the majority of the Firangis (foreigners), occupy yourself with nothing but dumb stones, vessels of brass, tiles and fabrics: contemplate the world of ideas, rather than the world of form and seek for truth rather than curiosities.'

The Muslim's plea to the visitor we mean to heed, in quest of 'truth, not curiosities', 'the world of ideas rather than the world of form'. Not that curiosity and the external form are to be abandoned, for without them we can scarcely penetrate to truth and idea. Fabric, tiles and not so dumb stones have their place and part in the student's apprehension of Islam. But we must abjure the type of curiosity that remains wholly within its own private world of reference and finds odd and weird whatever is not readily congenial and familiar. The curiosity for which there are only curiosities has not begun to be study. For it has not begun to transcend its own instinctive prejudice. Its ignorance is still the main criterion of its assessments.

23

'Gladly would I do as you advise,' Browne replied. 'I trust I am not so bigoted as to refuse fairly to consider whatever proofs can be adduced in favour of your religion.' Nor are we, in these pages, though it may be fair to observe that this particular protest of openmindedness moves rather too exclusively in the realm of external argument. 'Proofs' of religion are highly problematical at best, since the criteria of what has to be demonstrated, and how, are not readily agreed and still less readily attained. But for the present the response is fair enough. However, Browne continued: 'unfortunately your countrymen and co-religionists, so far from offering any facilities to unbelievers, would drive me from their shrines like a dog if I attempted to approach them.'[1]

Taken aback by the force of a fact which, in his exhortation, he had momentarily forgotten, the Persian could only admit its truth and urge the would-be orientalist to pursue his proper studies beneath the surface of Islam, with the somewhat dubious, if indispensable, device of personal disguise. Not a few western explorers and Islamicists have followed that suggestion, unable to seek the truth of Islam within the form, except by the untruth of a false external seeming of their own. Readers of Richard Burton's two-volumed *A Pilgrimage to Al-Madinah and Meccah* will remember the perpetual risks and the bold thoroughness of his Muslim impersonization of an Afghan 'doctor', 'one Abdallah, son of Yusuf, originally from Kabul'.

Today, except in the still impenetrable sanctuaries of Arabia, the case is different: the Muslim world is almost entirely open. How its accessibility would have amazed and delighted the author of *A Year among the Persians*. These seven decades later no disguise is necessary to penetrate the

[1] E. G. Browne, *A Year among the Persians*, Cambridge University Press, London, 1893, p. 274.

mosque and its fascinating world. The writer has left his shoes beside scores of portals from Tangier to Isfahan, in Ankara, Aligarh and Accra. Rarely has he been received with anything but courtesy and a ready welcome. With this openness to spur and test his sincerity, the student of today has inviting doors to meaning under form and reality beyond externals.

The will to explore, it is true, found stimulus in sheer adversity when massive external deterrents and perils provided a context of adventure. Burton and Doughty might find our scholarship too tame. But adventures enough remain and of a deeper, sounder, kind. The old traveller's tenacity, which made Doughty, undisguised in the Hijaz, so powerful a figure, can today be employed in the still formidable, if more prosaic, tasks of study and interpretation. Explorations of the spirit continue though the physical seclusions have so largely disappeared. The sturdy refusal to despair which carried the author of *Arabia Deserta* through interminable obstacles and dangers remains a necessary attitude for inward ventures of the mind. Physically the inquiring visitors of today move with the utmost ease – unless political considerations prevent – in most areas where Islam can be typically encountered (always excepting Islam within the Soviet Union and China). But spiritually we are far from matching the situation with patient ventures into understanding. Means of access across the wide world have far outrun our spiritual capacity to use them – and that, at a time when men and cultures must either co-exist or be co-extinct. If the wheel of a plane on a tarmac is one symbol of our age, perhaps a sandal beside a door can become another. Where there is deceptive ease of intercontinental travel, both for men and missiles, we need the honest pains of inter-cultural endeavour.

Some further reflections on the contemporary dimensions of this religious obligation to life will be discussed below in Part 2, where inter-religion is seen as both a physical fact and a spiritual problem. The purpose now is to see the significance of this Muslim openness, to picture it symbolically around the mosque door and to proceed upon it. That door, with its passage from a day-to-day Muslim existence into the meaning of Islam inside the mosque, will be our point of entry into 'the world of ideas'. The necessary courtesy of leaving our sandals there is simply a token of the exacting conditions of a Christian relationship to Islam. That the shoes of the Christian student mingle with those of the Muslim worshipper is no more than a sign of our human alongsidedness. If the former's are taken off with a somewhat self-conscious clumsiness that contrasts with the customary ease of the man who belongs there, this only provides an apt reminder of our difference.

It is uncertain when the Muslim practice of removing sandals before entering a mosque began. The famous historian, Al-Tabari, dates the custom from the reign of Umar, the second Caliph of Islam (A.D. 634–644). Other authorities suggest that it comes down from the second year after the Hijrah from Mecca to Medinah, around A.D. 624. But it is certain that the practice is very primitive and that it has origin in the general Semitic sense that a condition of shoelessness is a sacrament of reverence. One may compare Ex. 3.5: 'Put thy shoes from off thy feet, for the place whereon thou standest is holy ground.' Surah xx.12 reiterates this directive in its account of the story of Moses, though this is the only reference in the Quran.

It has been understood by some to indicate a laying aside of family and material pre-occupations or as a gesture expressing an intention to abide and remain, both of which may well carry over into similar usage at the mosque. It may be remarked that there is a widespread custom of leaving sandals outside Christian houses of worship in India. There is nothing exclusively Islamic about the habit, though Islam and the mosque are doubtless its most familiar example.

Here, then, at the mosque gate the sandals accumulate at the hour of prayer. Out of what are the worshippers coming, as they pass down the street into the sacred precincts? With what emotions do they cross the threshold into the court? What thoughts are uppermost in their minds? What brings them, besides the tradition of their heritage and the culture of their society? Has competition sharpened their fidelity or dulled it? Are the footsteps keen and eager, or only habitual and perfunctory? On what are they discoursing as they make their way through thronging city humanity or the intimates of village life? What questions are they asking themselves? What queries most properly fit the reverent outsider in contemplation of their actions and their antecedents, their coming in and going out? Here as in so many pursuits of scholarship and life, the fine art of knowledge is the fine art of wise inquiry. The response attempted here to such interrogation is only intended to help the reader to go on asking more thoroughly.

Complete and documentary answers on many issues would require an exhaustive treatise on the primitive origins, the long history and the contemporary fortunes of Islam and nice discussion of its theological development, its sociology and jurisprudence. Introductory handbooks to Islam for these purposes are happily available.[1]

---

[1] For example: H. A. R. Gibb, *Muhammadanism*, Oxford University Press, London, 2nd edition, 1953, and A. Guillaume, *Islam*, Penguin Books, London, 1954. See also the short bibliography below, pp. 155–160.

These pages are not set to reproduce them but to attempt a pattern of relationship with people, to walk with them in their shoes and understand them when they lay the shoes aside.

THE INTERPRETER'S PULPIT

Let us suppose it is the Muslim New Year, the opening of Al-Muharram, the month following the last in the calendar which is Dhu al-Hijjah, or month of pilgrimage. Most of the pilgrims are well on their way homeward or have already arrived and in their conversation are giving to their listening neighbours a vicarious experience of Mecca and its sacred environs. Al-Muharram, furthermore, is the month of the crowning Shiah recollection of the martyred Husain whom the tenth day pictures with dramatic ritual in the tragedy of Karbala.[1] The same tenth day, or thereabouts, brings to pious Sunnis the fast of Ashura, a religious festival ante-

---

[1] The distinction between Sunni and Shiah is the earliest, deepest and widest in Islam. Sunnis, the major element, are by definition the people of the Sunnah or 'way' of the Quran and the tradition. So, indeed, are Shiahs, though with three basic original and perpetual motives which distinguish them sharply from Sunnis. These are: (*a*) a political repudiation of the first three Caliphs, emerging into plain history in the reign of the third of these, Uthman, and a championing of the house of Ali, son-in-law and cousin of Muhammad and father of the Prophet's grandsons, Hasan and Husain; (*b*) after the violent deaths of the three Alids (the third, Husain, at the massacre of Karbala, A.D. 680), Shiah Islam found intense emotional meaning in the sense of innocent suffering and its relation to forgiveness. It also derived from this tradition of martyrdom a vivid ritual of remembrance in Muharram; (*c*) Shiah Islam holds a contrasted concept of the relation of the ongoing generations to the Quranic revelation. Whereas Sunnis believe in its perpetual accessibility in the custody of the community and its documents, Shiahs believe in its mediation through the Imams. The ramifications of these distinctions are not only very intricate and extensive but are integral to the whole ethos of Islam.

dating the month-long fast of Ramadan in Islam's ritual evolution. Also on a day of Al-Muharram the door of the Ka'bah, in the great Mosque in Mecca, is opened, in what we may take as still another symbol of our desire for valid insight. And yet again, Al-Muharram is traditionally the time of the original mandate for a Jerusalem Qiblah, or direction of prayer, for the infant Muslim community, years before it migrated to Medina and remembrance of Mecca took spiritual priority over Jerusalem. Al-Muharram is also the month when many Muslim landlords and tenants renew old tenancies or start new ones. Since there are so many new departures in today's Islam — political independence, economic change, movements of thought and society — it may be poetically just to think of it as living in a sort of perpetual Muharram, or, in the metaphor of the Latin 'January', facing both ways, standing at doors that are closing to open beyond. On this Muharram Friday we enter and listen to the sermon.

The preacher is Ahmad ibn Abdallah.

In the Name of God, the merciful Lord of mercy. Praise be to God Who has made time to consist of years and has divided years into months and days, in accordance with His supreme wisdom and design and has opened every year with this month of Al-Muharram and made it memorable with the day of Ashura, great and honoured, whose excellence was known and celebrated both in the time of ignorance and under Islam.

I praise Him, the ever-praised, the exalted and I give Him thanks. I ask His pardon and I seek His mercy upon all that by the fates has happened. I repent in His sight and I bear witness that there is no god save God alone: He has no partner and is exalted above all association and resemblance and above all that can be conceived by mind or conscience.

And I bear witness that our lord Muhammad is His servant, His apostle, His friend and loyal beloved, by the shining lamp of whose guidance God has directed His people. May God bless and preserve this noble Prophet, the praised one, the great apostle of our Lord and our pattern, Muhammad. May He likewise bless and preserve his people and his most excellent followers.

O ye people, here is a new year come upon you. Pay honour, then, to what it brings. It comes to alert and awaken you, so be ready to greet it in a like spirit. Tirelessly it brings you its warning call. Indeed there is not a day that passes but what summons you in its own way and speaks out of its own significance.

And I too call to every one of you, by the nearness of his departing hour. Let each be prepared for his journey to the abode of destiny. You who are happy by the renewal of the years and find pleasure in the coming of the new moons and the flux of the days, you must have realized how they shorten your limited span. Then take heed, poor fellow, this world is a confusion of dreams, a transient abode where there is no abiding. Let it be to you as if it were a shining full moon eclipsed. Be busied in this month of yours with good works, be much in abstinence and purify your intention in word and deed. Be warned against corrupting things, for truly the Accounter is vigilant. Bring forth alms of what you have and do not fear to give it out of want. For almsgiving, as we have been reminded by the preacher-warner, does not lead to impoverishment.

It is recorded of the faithful Prophet, the just one (may the blessing and the peace of God be upon him), that he said: After the stipulated prayers, the best prayer is the night prayer and the best fast after Ramadan is the fast of Al-Muharram, the month of God. God has made us worthy, you and I, God has made us worthy to perceive the glories of His revelation. He has fitted us to perform the behest of His commands and to reap the fruits of His good pleasure.

The greatest thing to which men of good heart are exhorted and the noblest thing to which a wise penitent is guided is the word of God, whereunto whosoever clings, as to a rope, he will not be destitute. For God the most high says: By his word shall the guided be guided. When the Quran is read listen to it, listen to it in silence, it may be you will find mercy. I take refuge with God from the accursed Satan.

30

The number of months with God is twelve, according to God's book, on the day when He created the heavens and the earth. Four of them are sacred. That is the true religion. In them do not wrong your souls. Fight to an end with the idolaters just as they resist you to the end and know that God is with the righteous. In the mighty Quran God has greatly blessed both you and me. He has granted us the favour of His signs, the recollection whereof is prudent. He accepts from me and from you the recital of it, for He both knows and hears.

I enjoin upon you, as upon myself, as servants of God, piety towards Him. Good success is to the God-fearing. The Quran urges you and me to be obedient unto God and His apostle at all times. It may be that you will have good prosperity. I ask forgiveness of God most high, for myself and for you, for my parents and your parents and for the rest of the Muslims, both men and women and believers of both sexes. Do you also ask forgiveness of Him. For He is the deliverance of the pardon seekers and the salvation of the penitent.[1]

Is the sermon typical? the reader may inquire. Would it be fair to reply with a counter query whether anything is truly typical? There is, for example, nothing political in the sermon, nor anything scientific. It does not enjoin a reverent use of reason or claim all truth for Islam in the realm of modern science. It makes no comment on the problems that result from technology. Nor does it castigate secular influences or warn against their inroads. Perhaps in these respects the discourse is a little old-fashioned, while its references to time have to be read in the light of the new year season. It is nevertheless as typical as the preacher's name. What matters more is whether it is Islamic and on that score there can be no doubt.

Here are the characteristic themes and phrases of Muslim devotion and exhortation: 'Seeking refuge with God'; 'Asking

[1] Translated from Ahmad ibn Abdallah, *Al-Khutab-al Wa'iziyyah*, Bombay edition, n.d.

for pardon'; 'the purifying of the intention' and 'recollection of God's signs'; or, in Quranic terms, the *Tawidh*, the *Istighfar*, the *Niyyah*, *Dhikr* and *Ayat*. Running through it is the sense of corporate belonging and the privileged custody of final revelation. Here too is the matchless boon of the Quran and the obligation to trustful fulfilment of religious duty. And over all is that most representative of Muslim attitudes towards God, namely *Taqwa* – a piety that gathers into itself awe, watchfulness, dignity and discipline. It is the only fully valid form of acknowledgment of God. Such *Taqwa* has for centuries informed the Muslim soul. It sometimes discloses itself even in demeanour and countenance. In all these senses the preacher is clue enough and his sermon a clear mirror of Islam.

Nor is this the end of its value, taken thus at random, as an epitome of Islam. It opens, of course, with the *Bismillah* or invocation of the name of God with the sacred, double descriptive: 'In the Name of the merciful Lord of mercy' – an invocation which embodies devotionally what Islam proclaims dogmatically. 'There is none save He' in fact: 'none save He' in prayer. This is the phrase which prefaces every Surah in the Quran save Surah ix where its absence, though a mystery, is not significantly strange. With these words the new-born are greeted, the departing hallowed and the occasions of life, whether minor like a schoolboy's new copybook or major like the making of a marriage or the founding of a state, are solemnized and blessed.

The double adjectives *Al-Rahman al-Rahim* relate to the mercy of God as a property or attribute of His nature and a constantly operative quality of His relationship to man. Because He is the *Rahman*, He acts as the *Rahim*. The ultimate in the mercy of God is the fact of Islam, the benediction of this honoured community with whom revelation has come to its climax and the favour of God to its crowning purpose. Here too is the sense of 'the people of God' who are such in being also 'the people of the Prophet' joining together in their very status that intimate relation between God and His apostle which is credally affirmed in the *Shahadah*, or Confession of belief.

Yet this community has no grounds for presumption or arrogance. It must ever repent, confess, struggle, countering the foes of God, until they desist and God is all. It must remember its obligation to devotion, the Pillars of its religion, its Ramadan – the best of fasts – and its almsgiving – the clue to its social obligations. For in Zakat, or payment of alms, is to be seen that acknowledgment of the right of God and of society in the possessions of the propertied which validates their ownership. By token consecration of the part, they cleanse and hallow the whole. By paying to the Divine community, they legitimize what they retain. Recognition of 'not mine' in the fact of wealth validates my calling it 'mine'. So let Muslims be assiduous in almsgiving, for the Lord does not approve those who withhold their giving out of fear of poverty. This is a mistaken calculus. The fulfilment of religious duty is always a condition of true prosperity: it is niggardliness which impoverishes. Cannot God blight and scatter what we selfishly preserve? Can He not multiply and fructify what we willingly give up? Has not the whole history of the community of the faith demonstrated that God is never in debt to an obedient people?

There is history, too, as well as implied economics, in the sermon. God presides over time. But He does more than divide it into years and months and days. He does not merely order a calendar and sanctify the sacred months for the education and discipline of the God-fearing. He also orders and dominates its pattern of events. In Muslim perspective this is surely seen in the contrast between the days of faith and that *Jahiliyyah* or era of polytheism, prior to Islam, when Arabia lay in the darkness of ignorance. Then was that fear of poverty, against which the preacher just gave warning. In the *Jahiliyyah* fear made men miserly and bellicose. Life was 'nasty, brutish and short': nasty in its heathenish practices, brutish in its untaught uncouthness and short in its feuding and war. Such was the 'Time of Ignorance', the darkness before the dawn – a time which in some historians and sermonizers is blackened into a heinousness that does not justly describe it. Our preacher recognizes that the roots of the Ashura go back into these pre-Islamic times. There were in dispersion in Arabia colonies of 'the people of the Book', Jews and Christians, from whose Scriptures and rituals the nascent faith drew deeply both of inspiration and example.

Though he does not mention them, Ahmad ibn Abdallah knows well of the Hanifs. (For what preacher is it who with this admirable brevity can tell you all a faith?) These men of incipient monotheism, after their great prototype, Abraham himself, had reached out hopefully from the idolatry and polytheism of their fellow countrymen, towards the liberating purity of a monotheistic faith. Theirs, it would appear, was something of the nausea at idolatry that possessed the soul of Muhammad in the days of the genesis of his original mission on Mount Hira. From their example and stimulus came in part the historical factors that cradled the earliest Islam.

The significant difference between the Prophet and the Hanifs lay in the fact that monotheism came to him as a personal crusading mission and welded, through his prophet-hood, a political and social unity for Arabia. Yet even so, in the new heritage and dispensation, there came down from the Jewish past ritual legacies, fasts and feasts, or the idea of them, calendars and times, to be observed in the devotional interests of corporate religion. Even then in the *Jahiliyyah*, as the sermon has it, the shape of Islam was being fashioned in the providence of the all-seeing God. For it was not essentially a new faith, in the sense of a totally unprecedented thing. What is new is the completeness, so it is believed, of the monotheism, its custody in the ultimate community and its perfect expression in the culminating revelation. But all anticipatory intimations of it, in the heroic individualism of Abraham, the compromised heritage of the Jews and the distorted beliefs of those other Scriptuaries – the Christians – are preserved authentically and embodied securely in the new allegiance.

Muhammad is the seal of the prophets, the apex of prophethood, the last in the succession which begins with Adam who, having 'words' given to him wherewith to name the creatures, really started all science. For until a thing is named it cannot come into the currency of knowledge. The message of this long series of prophets is essentially one, particularized to time and place and tribe. In Muhammad prophecy comes not only to its ultimate term but to its universal range. In the Quran, though admittedly an Arabic document (with its Arabic quality an inalienable part of its status as the Divine word), and therefore not readily accessible to all, is the revelation to end revelation.

When the preacher refers to 'the people of the Prophet' he includes not only the present generation, dispersed in the world, but the sequence of all the generations in the *Islam* before Islam. He salutes a progeny that has a retrospect beyond Abraham and a prospect beyond Christ. Hence the assurance with which Islam is to meet and resist all opposition to these claims. The whole meaning of the struggle to which our sermon refers lies in the claim of Islam to an inclusive finality that is also exclusive. It is inclusive in the totalitarian

35

sense of being hostile to partialities and opposites, demanding from all a submissive integration into itself. Yet by the same token it claims that all such integration is simply the fulfilment of all that is elsewhere valid.

Here lies the clue to the distinction between *Dar al-Islam* and *Dar al-Harb* – the household of submission and the household of resisters. The gainsayers who perpetuate the spirit of Mecca's original opponents of the Prophet are like them to be brought into submission. The logic of the early history is the logic of the whole history of Islam. *Dar al-Harb* is the realm that has not yet admitted the final right of Islam. It cannot be allowed to maintain its resistance unchallenged. For then Islam would be disloyal to its inner conviction of finality. This concept of the household of Islam is a sublime kind of intolerance, the faith to see the whole world in its own image and to serve the fulfilment of the vision. Since it believes that fulfilment is attainable under proper external conditions and in terms of politics, the state, education and the law, it resolves that such conditions shall at all costs be realized. This is the ideological meaning of *Dar al-Islam*, the will to the extension of the empire of Islam.

It is also the underlying philosophy of the *Jihad* of which our Ahmad ibn Abdallah reminds his listeners, some of them lately back from pilgrimage, where they have partaken of the sacrament of universality. Christianity likewise has the courage of universal convictions. But believing that the conditions of their realization are more than external and political it cannot properly identify one part of the world as its actual household and the other part as otherwise occupied territory. On the contrary any division of humanity deriving from Christ belongs to the hearts of persons as persons. Though territories as such can be relatively permeated with or denuded of such persons, there can be no ultimate territorial expression of the Gospel. Rather it creates its own inter-penetrating community – the *ecclesia* – whose badge is the new heart and suffering – a community that lives in grace, recognizes the law and grows by a spiritual contagion. It neither founds states, nor disowns them, but, leavening all it can for truth and purity, confesses that the leavening element is not the whole.

The Islamic *Jihad* is the struggle against all that is antithetical to the truth of Islam. Though traditionally imperial, it has also taken on a spiritual and inward meaning. The truly surrendered one is called upon to struggle and toil for the actualization of the Islamic ideal. The foes are then, not only, or so much, other peoples and territories, but wrongs, evils, injustices and inequalities. The *Jihad* becomes an ideological enterprise with the goal, not of political empire, but of a true society. Since the latter must, in the end, consist of true persons, the struggle becomes inward and private. The enemies are seen to be the temptations of the inner man, the sloth, pride, self-seeking and complacence that impede a personal Islam. Against these 'Quraish of the heart'[1] the proper Muslim must war until the end, having no truce or truck with any private antitheses of his Muslim vocation. So at least many of the mystics have taught and much recent sociological realism has begun to recognize,[2] even though it would be unwise to suppose that all the preacher's hearers give his exhortation this interpretation.

[1] Quraish were the Meccan community from whom the Prophet came but who also were his most inveterate enemies prior to his conquest of the city. So they are taken here as a synonym for antipathy to the good.

[2] Cf. Abd al-Nasir, *Falsafat al-Thaurah* (The Philosophy of the Revolution), Cairo, 1953, in which the President of Egypt reflected upon the need for 'unselfish Egyptians' as the greatest single contribution to the success of the then new regime.

One of his phrases more than any other might sustain, if not actually suggest, these ruminations. There is no passing day, says he, but speaks to men (literally) 'with the tongue of its condition', or, as rendered in our translation, 'speaks out of its own significance'. Here also no doubt the potential apprehension is wider than the actual. Every day has its peculiar circumstances and addresses man therein. But is there not also in this magnificent phrase a charter of wider relevance? The days, which in their dawning herald the glory of God, speak also in their historical unfolding to receptive man. With what voice does atomic 'day' speak to the world? How do the present discontents speak to their contemporaries? What is the 'word of the living God' vocal for us in the far-ranging meanings of our contemporary history?

Islam is not an outmoded ideology. Its basic principle of God's proper worship and of idolatry's wretchedness (all idolatries, be they disguised in ideologies or metamorphosed into systems, political or economic) demand an ever-fresh articulation for the guidance of modern man. For 'by His word shall the guided be guided' – the phrase is not merely repetitious. The guided ones are not somehow to be left perplexed. 'Cursed be he', said a tradition of the Prophet, 'who removeth the landmarks.' There is no lostness so real as that which cannot read the familiar and irreplaceable directions. The *Furqan* (as one name of the Quran has it), then, the revealed criterion, must be currently applied. Its relevance must be up to date. The heirs of the guidance must know how to read it lest they become misguided, not for want of an authority but from lack of its immediate direction.

THE SERMON AND DEVOTION

We may question whether Ahmad ibn Abdallah had all this in mind. But the silence of preachers is often eloquent enough, if their phrases have a potential beyond their occasion. This ever-vigilant awareness of the contemporary meaning of the age-long involves certain practical issues, to which we shall turn later. Meanwhile we are still with the listening throng, the tradesmen and the artisans, the lawyers, clerks and students, the workers and peasants, who occupy the broad spaces of the mosque, mingling in the commonalty of Islam and shortly to engage in their most unifying and expressive ritual – the *Salat*.

For the sermon, above all else, is leading into worship. Its notions and phrases are all to that end. It comes itself, usually, between the second and the third repetitions of the *Adhan* or call to prayer. The first has occurred at the outset, from the minaret. During it the faithful have duly gathered, leaving aside our symbol their sandals. The second followed it from inside the mosque, perhaps intoned by the *Khatib* or preacher himself (though generally in any sizable mosque the functions are divided among the official personnel). When the preacher concludes, the call will be repeated and the prostrations and ascriptions will begin, according to the careful and strict sequence of prostration known as a *Rakah*. The preacher's own formal phrases of praise, with which he traditionally opens and concludes his discourse, are an over-ture of the *Sujud*.[1] 'I praise God': 'I ask His forgiveness': 'I bear witness that Muhammad is His apostle' – these are the 'confessions' of the Muslim. The pulpit, as it were, antici-pates the congregation.

It does so also in other ways. In all sermons Quranic memoriter plays a large part. Ahmad ibn Abdallah is obviously no exception. In rehearsing certain familiar

[1] *Sujud* is the term applied to that part of the sequence of prayer movements in which the brow is in contact with the prayer mat, or with a tiny stone laid on it.

passages or alluding to them, like 'the rope of God' (Surah iii.103) and 'the shining lamp' (Surah xxiv.35), he exemplifies what he enjoins. For the Quran above all else exists to be recited and so also to have constant auditors. It occupies both the tongue and the ear, the voice and the mind. When it is chanted, the soul of Muslim music speaks. Where calligraphy inscribes it, we find the soul of Muslim art. The devout must listen in silence, seeking refuge from the accursed devil. For in an activity as sacred as recitation evil is like to be intrusive and must be rigorously forestalled. Did not the accursed Satan endeavour, unsuccessfully, to throw in dubious and mistaken phrases, when the Prophet was hearing and reciting the sacred text (Surah xxii.52)? Will he not seek likewise to snatch away, to distort, disfigure and discredit, the word passing precariously from the tongue of the chanter to the ear and spirit of the hearer?

Such is the Muslim reverence for the written and uttered word that the time of this transaction is invested with peculiar wonder and peculiar peril. Seeking refuge from the accursed devil is like the cross-making, or holy water sprinkling, of certain Christians in the presence of what is peculiarly sacred in the faith and ritual. The mosque in Islam is not a place of material superstition, unless so degraded by the presence of relics, tombs and charms in a context of animism or impure Sufism. But the occasion of Quranic recitation is an occasion of the numinous and must be so guarded and regarded.

The use of the *Tasliyah*,[1] which Ahmad ibn Abdallah also exemplifies, can be explored in this same context. His

---

[1] The term that describes the invocation here discussed. It is by derivation the verbal noun from the first verb of the phrase, meaning: 'Saying *Salla* etc.'

On the *Tasliyah*, see Constance E. Padwick, *The Muslim World*, vol. xlvii, 1, Jan. 1957, pp. 5–16, 'The Language of Muslim Devotion'.

references to the name and status of Muhammad are followed at once by the traditional words: *Salla Allahu alaihi wa Sallam* – which may be rendered, 'May God grant blessing upon him and preserve him in peace.' The two verbs used, referring to God, are past tenses in the optative, having the sense of invocation. 'May it be', when God responds, is as good as already done. The first verb belongs to the root which gives the term for ritual prayer or worship, *Salat*. It is not, however, to be understood that God is being desired to bring Muhammad worship – an inconceivable thought. It is that God Himself recognizes the central and unique place of Muhammad in the Divine economy of revelation and is called upon to do so by the community the revelation fashions. On their side it is an act of recognition of their standing and *raison d'être*: on His part it is the perpetuating of the eternal fact of Muhammad's role as Islam sees it. God, as it were, at the behest of this generation of Muslims, for ever authenticates the status of that prophethood which shapes all the generations.

The phrase is based upon Surah xxxiii.56: 'Verily God and His angels send down blessing upon the Prophet. O ye who believe call down blessing upon him and greet him with peace.' God's action is taken to mean the magnifying of the Prophet, though there are suggestions in the commentator Al-Baidawi and elsewhere that God's *Salat* means forgiveness. In general it is the sense of God's satisfaction with Muhammad which predominates. It is even hinted in some quarters that only God is truly able to exalt and celebrate the Prophet, as men, being full of failings and evil, cannot worthily do. Their *Salat* upon the Prophet becomes a plea for acceptance with God and a recognition of the terms of their spiritual education. It is also possible to find a mystical connotation to the whole phrase and think of the eternal joy of God in the initiative of His revelatory grace. But whatever the final significance there is no more characteristic phrase in Muslim devotion. The *Tasliyah* has come to be inseparable from the whole prayer rite and to epitomize the religious status of the Prophet in popular Islam.

That status as a historical memory is the gist of Tradition – the vast corpus of communal recollection which, after the Quran, is the second source of Muslim jurisprudence. Our sermon is loyal to its true patterns in quoting, albeit sparingly, from the sayings and deeds of the Prophet. For the mosque discourse is one of the main means for the currency of Tradition. The preacher will find almost inexhaustible material for the elaboration and illustration of his exhortations, in the *obiter dicta*, the anecdotes and experiences of the Prophet and his companions. Just as, in the technical phrase, the traditionalist had his *isnad*, or chain of attestation (on which he, literally, 'leans') so the preacher or *khatib* leans heavily upon these collections of canonical traditions, in which communal memory refreshes itself in prophetic example.

The times and circumstances in which the saying arose, or the anecdote occurred, may well differ widely from those to which today's mosque hearer belongs or to which the contemporary pulpit applies them. It is possible, for example, to reinforce the theories of the welfare state from a narrative of how the Prophet disapproved some attempted monopoly of well or pasture, or to validate the pursuits of the modern laboratory by Muhammad's commendation of eager copyists of holy words. Yet these quotations from Tradition are the form of mediation of the past. In mediated history is continuity. The preacher by his use of them sets the hearer's world in the dimensions of the faith's heritage and that no doubt is his proper function.

The other direction of the hortatory setting is prospective

and eschatological. Here, too, Ahmad ibn Abdallah is representative. Islam was a faith in a Divine legislation for mankind which looked onward to the vivid reality of Judgment. The law was to be no idle letter. The adversaries were under sentence. Only repentance could avail. Time was the crucial setting of this decision and time was running out. On this note the preacher re-echoes the strident emphases of the early preaching the Quran records. The passion of Muhammad's portrayal of that impending grand assize has gone from today's *minbar*: 'The calamity, the calamity, would that you knew what that calamity is' (Surah ci.1–2)! But in word, if not in urgent vehemence, the conviction remains that so characterizes the Quran. God is a God of judgment. The last reckoning will tell. The scales will rigorously test the deeds of men. Woe unto those whose scales are light (Surah ci.8).

Our thoughts prolong themselves beyond the limits of the sermon itself. But only as other sermons might. These at any rate are the characteristic notes of mosque discourse. Had we visited another mosque, or chanced upon another preacher, or chosen another Friday, these pages might have differed somewhat in their contents. Unless we make abstractions and analyses our goal – and how dull they are as a treatment of living immensities – we had to choose a particular mosque on a particular Friday, testing our particular experience by such generalizations as books and longer acquaintance and encounter may provide. Checked by such criteria there can be little doubt that Ahmad ibn Abdallah, within the limits of a single discourse, has proved a valid mentor. As a preacher he shows no personal idiosyncrasies that disqualify him from being representative. We may be reasonably certain that we have sampled the mosque sermon. The portals where the sandals lie lead into this world within.

CONGREGATIONAL REFLECTIONS

But have we in fact found Islam? Is this the end of our quest? Have we now the answers to our interrogation? Or must we wrestle with the uneasy suspicion that perhaps the mosque sermon is not our proper quarry? Agreeing that this sermon, as well as any, mirrors mosque Islam, have we been precipitate in supposing that it gives us all we need to know the Muslim? Are we taking Ahmad too seriously, more eagerly, perhaps, than his own hearers? Did we hasten inwards to listen, with insufficient sense of the Muslims who show no such eagerness for the words of the *minbar*? Was it a right assumption that the sermon would be our best clue?

Hurry we certainly did. For we had no sooner parted with our sandals than we were attending to the preacher. We bypassed the ablutions in which every Muslim prepares himself for ritual prayer. The cleansing of the more exposed members of the body, right side and then left, is a sacrament of personal belonging and symbolizes the purity true prayer requires. Although we gave it no attention, this feature is part of the devotion of committed people. Perhaps too our hopeful entry into 'the world of ideas' failed sufficiently to notice the absentees. For ritual ablutions focus and express an attitude of symbolic incorporation into Islamic meanings which the dubious and the sceptical are unwilling to allow. For washing oneself personalizes one's allegiance when performed in ritual context on the threshold of worship. What, then, of the people who are rarely, if ever, in the mosque court, whose normal significance is just in being absentees? In simplest terms, is the mosque, as articulate in its preachers, the whole of Islam?

It must be noted here that as far as prayer, even ritual

prayer, is concerned in Islam mosques are dispensable. Wherever he chooses the believer may address his Creator and witness to his Prophet, making an immediate sanctuary of his personal prayer mat. On Fridays at noon, however, and at other times and days where convenient, the mosque is proper. Absence from congregational prayer on 'the day of gathering' is a religious failure in duty. Then at least the mosque population should be identical with the believing community, at least of menfolk, excepting travellers, the aged and infirm.

These, however, are far from being all the absentees whose non-attendance we remark. But before seeking out those for whom the mosque is intellectually uncongenial it is necessary to ponder briefly the prevailing absence of womenfolk – a feature of the average mosque that is always puzzling to the foreign observer. The reasons go very far back into the attitudes and traditions of Islam. The overwhelming preponderance of men in Muslim acts of worship should not lead the student to hasty conclusions of essential inequality in the sexes before God. Surah xxxiii.34–35 is the only occasion in the Quran (save Surah lxvi.5 where the context concerns only the Prophet's wives) of the use of the feminine plural *Muslimat*, meaning 'Muslim women'. Frequently, of course, the masculine *Muslimun* has a common sense and must be held, at least by implication, to include both sexes. But the passage cited, though unique, carefully inserts the feminine plural counterpart of every masculine it uses: 'surrendered ones', 'believers', 'devout, sincere, patient worshippers', 'payers of alms', 'keepers of the fast', 'chaste folk' and 'rememberers of God'. In every case these categories are specifically feminized so that there may be no doubt that the vocation of Islam, both in faith and practice, in creed and temper, belongs without distinction to both sexes. This verse, and the one that follows, setting all believers 'both men and women' under obligation of steady conformity to the will of God and His Prophet, are a final authority on the question of the involvement of women in Islam.

But social conventions and actual usages, from the earliest times, have tended to make the public mosque the haunt of men alone. Surah xxxiii.33 enjoins the Prophet's wives to 'stay in their homes' and 'attend to their prayers'. While other women were not under the necessity of seclusion to the degree the immediate household was, the tendency inevitably was for its ways to become exemplary. The principles the Quran itself laid down strictly limiting social intercourse and enjoining careful avoidance by women of male society outside a closely defined circle of near relatives all tended to encourage the practice of private prayer on women's part and to discourage the use of the general mosques.

In many of these, it is true, areas of the interior were judiciously screened or divided so that women could engage in devotional acts in a setting that immunized them from unwonted male attentions. From the Quran onwards this instinct for privacy has made the mosque in large measure a male preserve and since devotional realms are the slowest to yield to change the new emergence of women has not yet, by and large, reflected itself in the mosque picture. There is also a widespread feeling of the female being taken for granted in the male, not unlike the way it happens in verbs and nouns. When the Egyptian feminist leader, Doria Shafiq, invited the Egyptian (all male) Parliament to explain in 1950 how it could call itself 'representative' when it omitted, both in membership and in the suffrage behind it, the female half of the nation, the obvious answer was that the male half *was* the political whole, within which the female half was already vicariously represented, just as the children were. In something of the same way, general standards of opportunity and education as well as prevailing social norms assisting, Muslim men in the mosque have a sort of unwritten but real 'family' capacity. The *Muslimat* are there so to speak by male implication. Feminine discontent with this vicarious posture has not yet become articulate for the simple but sufficient reason that, in the modern fashion of the world, there are more urgent areas of feminine assertion over against more sensitive reaches of male monopoly. Meanwhile there are still the private *zawiyas*, or special courts, where the devotion of the Muslim women finds its secluded occasions, within earshot of the *minbar*, and beyond the range of the feminist concerns as they are asserted in the secular world.

That world it is which brings us back to the absentees who are male. Like other faiths of men, Islam is struggling with the inroads of secularity and indifference, though these in the nature of the case are not readily to be measured in statistics. The impulse to mosque attendance varies with the occasion. At notable landmarks of the year or of the state, it mounts: on more humdrum occasions of religious continuity it falls. The sources and fervour of the will to be present oscillate and change, perhaps in part, though less maybe than in Christianity, on grounds of the adequacy or otherwise of the religious personnel. There are classes in the community less readily, or less enthusiastically, in the mosque than others. Not that the externals of Islam are neglected, for they have an important emotional role in contemporary nationalism and reform. A crowded mosque with its attentive, reverent overflow of worshippers on to the streets outside, is a frequent sight in Muslim cities. But for some at least the world of the laboratory, the bank, the university, seems to consort unevenly, even incongruously, with that other world of chant and prostration.

It is partly, our critical neighbours beside the mosque pillar might observe, the education and consequent mental make-up of the man to whom we have just listened. He preaches well enough for a Muharram of the past centuries, even of the nineteenth century. But he has allowed himself to be left behind by the newness of the present years. Doubtless by his education he really knows his faith, as we, his Muslim critics, hardly do. He is fully conversant with the margins of his Quran, where the commentators abound. He can recite freely, as we cannot, both the sacred text and the sacrosanct Bukhari, our renowned traditionalist. He can discourse upon the niceties of exegesis and indicate the issues between Al-Ghazali and Ibn Rushd in their famous *Tahafut* or disintegration controversy.[1] But to us, the real

[1] *Tahafut*. A major theme in Islamic theology is popularly indicated by this word *Tahafut* or 'Disintegration through Refutation'. It really means 'argumentatively expedited collapse' of schools of thought understood. Al-Ghazali (A.D. 1059–1111) used it in the title of his most famous philosophical work *Tahafut al-Falasifah* ('The Refutation of the Philosophers') written around 1095, in which he propounded a metaphysical scepticism. He insisted that the source of theology must be strictly religious or Scriptural, not rational. (Hence his tremendous feeling for the significance of religious experience revealed in his greatest theological treatise – *Ihya Ulum al-Din*.) Al-Ghazali disavowed the Muslim Aristotelians, like Al-Farabi and Ibn Sina, asserting that their arguments were unproven and discrediting the classical concepts of causality and the eternity of matter. Later Ibn Rushd (1126–1198) came to the defence of the philosophers and in his *Tahafut al-Tahafut* or 'Refutation of the Refutation' (written after 1180) re-asserted the familiar argument with a long and forceful summary of the controversy. He called Al-Ghazali 'the renegade of philosophy'. For a brief summary of the *Tahafut* controversy see George F. Hourani, 'The Dialogue between Al-Ghazali and the Philosophers on the Origin of the World', *The Muslim World*, vol. xlviii, 3 and 4, July and Oct. 1958, pp. 183–191 and 308–314.

Tahafut is the incohesion of the whole realm of theological dogma. That which to the pundits seems secure and un-questionable appears to us at once both assertive and in-secure. It strikes us as a dubious, if not also a somewhat despicable, refuge for the modern soul. Truly our preacher is aware of his Islam as a heritage and a retrospect, in a way that we, with our science and secularity, are not. But is he truly aware of it as a present reality, adequate to the prospects of twentieth-century man? Has he grappled with how, as well as with what, to believe?

It is his background, continues the critic, that disturbs and deters us – his university tradition, his approach to truth, his unalert dogmatism, his refuge without knowing it in plati-tude and sentiment. He does not feel the world as we feel it. Nor does he face the problems attaching to a true surrender to God in the world of high finance, of complex public administration or of international diplomacy. He has indeed harnessed modern techniques to his external needs. Have we not electronic amplification of our call to prayer? Radio from this very mosque gives our Ahmad ibn Abdallah a reach of audience that would have amazed his predecessors on this ancient *minbar*. But he and his kind have hardly yet begun to think or speak in the forms of thought that are valid and adequate to our time. They have not yet amplified and enlarged the reach of their souls into the life of their listeners.

Unless we quite unwarrantably compartmentalize our lives, leaving religion and dogma immune from the criticism – even from the curiosity – of the minds that come into action in our technology and our politics, we shall find in-creasing strain in our allegiance. We shall not lightly abandon it. For with what shall we replace it? We know that some-thing must do duty for the whole dimension of our finitude

D

and its mystery, giving them communal and symbolical expression. Though we may be secularized in behaviour, we would not be secular in our innermost souls. Are we not Muslims and as Muslims so speak? It may be that we are wrong in requiring religion to be intellectually accountable, and in despising it when it is not. But meanwhile we are ill at ease and cannot acquiesce in a cult we have neither the closed mind blindly to approve nor the proud heart blandly to repudiate. We are religious – but religiously perplexed. We are still Muslims. But we are not content to leave with the preacher the definition of our Islam, and we are uneasy about the way he represents it.

The fault is not wholly, not mainly, his. He and his way of expression are the result of a longstanding educational duality in our society. We have in fact, goes on our spokesman, two streams of education. The one is modern, scientific, state-controlled, professional. It proceeds by standards of critical scholarship, has no reservations of dogma, is amenable to evidence and verifies its hypotheses. It concerns itself with history, nature, society and politics, and of course all the sciences. It is progressive, empirical, and on the move. The other stream is traditional, dogmatic, mosque-centred, 'shaikhly'. It moves within the criteria of exegesis, reserves its sacrosanct territories and relies upon authorities. Its confidence is in retrospect. It concerns itself with the Quran, the Tradition, the Shariah, grammar and rhetoric. It is authoritarian, deductive and on the defensive. All too little do the streams flow together.

It is true that large strides have been taken in the modernization of curricula, buildings and student conditions. But it takes a longer time and patience to modernize the prepossessions. So the mosque pulpit still tends to be a mirror of the minds of its occupants and in turn of the pattern of their education. We are still awaiting, for example, a firmly established science of Quranic study, free from bondage to the old canons and masters of exegesis. Some tentative efforts have been made to explore the origins of Quranic terms and by comparative study to elucidate the many fascinating problems, not so much of text as of context, which belong to our sacred book.

Meanwhile, adds our commentator, this whole situation has reacted subtly upon the official custodians themselves. They have seen the world pass imperceptibly away from their recognized control. It is so often the products of the scientific culture who command the leadership, while the shaikhs tend for the most part to be left with a role and status among us far from commensurate with the devotion, the length and the carefulness of their studies. The younger among them find serious disquiet in this situation and react in a variety of ways, like men who feel deprived of the opportunity they have deserved to invest their training in careers that will really shape society and deserve the community's esteem. This problem of relative frustration can on occasion have obvious financial and material aspects also, which still further complicate its incidence and its solution. There are movements which propose a vigorous if not violent reassertion but which are for the most part held in check by the dominant 'lay' elements.

'Seek the world of ideas', said the Persian teacher. Our imaginary response to his advice has brought us very far in. As the mosque congregation moves in silence into the corporate prayer that begins with the ending of the sermon, it is time for a few reflections of our own. It begins to look as if we were rightly led in making our way there in search of Islam. For that Islam is revealed in both the custodians and the critics of the mosque. We apparently had a right clue in settling down to attend to a sermon. Even those least disposed to listen to the *minbar* are part of the totality to which, if not for which, it speaks.

The things which give some Muslims pause about shaikhs and sermons, mosques and *minbars*, are not to be crudely dismissed as irreligion. Doubtless that exists, as in all societies. Secularism, including the total Communist repudiation of the supernatural, is a potent and pervasive danger to which some have succumbed. Materialism, in the practical if not the philosophical sense, is a persuasive fashion, the harder to resist because of the invasions and successes of technology. Some conformity to religion is probably, in all cultures, materialist at heart. Chaucer's Pardoner, trading on men's inclination to pay lip service to doctrines and rituals they do not really revere, or to contract out of spiritual dues by worldly payments, is *mutatis mutandis* a universal phenomenon. Al-Hariri in his *Maqamat* described his Muslim equivalent. Yet when all this is rightly said, it is false and futile to dub all criticism of the establishment, be it mosque or church, as irreligious and profane. The ecclesiastical or the 'shaikhly' mind has too often been too prone to miss the wind of the Spirit 'blowing where it listeth' and to esteem all opposition to institutions as opposition to God.

We have, then, to see the *bona fide* critic as still a Muslim and the dubiety as within Islam, even though the conservative apologists dispute this. It follows that there is a living discussion implicitly in progress as to the very nature of Islam. It is not only we as Christian fellow-men who are 'in quest of Islam'. Muslims are. The sandals they leave at the gate are not only or always 'sandals of assurance' but 'sandals of aspiration'. There is a 'Whither?' as well as a 'Hither' about them. They belong to a community on the move because it is alive in modernity. Islam, in fine, is a tremendous ideology in religious form and, as we must see more closely in Part 3, is dominated by the concept of the rule of God over the whole of life. The demands of this rule are laid down in the given revelation. The whole system of faith, practice and behaviour, is designed to teach, actualize and perpetuate the responsive obedience. In all the bewildering confusion of the modern world, it would be odd if such an ideal did not encounter massive obstacles and raise profound issues as to what it really means in spirit and in fact.[1]

Our quest of Islam will surely proceed most wisely if we aim to follow the Muslim's own – and that in relation to three underlying questions: What is this Islam? Who is qualified to say? and How is it to be?

That there is properly a question as to what Islam is has already been illustrated by the critic's comments on the sermon. That the questions: What is distinctive and essential to the faith and practice of Islam? and What makes the authentic Muslim? are valid even the conservative must admit. It is true that he believes he already has the answers. But at least he has to defend and assert them and this involves him in all issues.

He doubtless believes too that all the data of the genuine Islam are indubitably known and accessible in the Quran and the Sunnah. A group of 'ulama' in Baghdad recently protested strongly to the writer that it was not the business of

[1] Nowhere has the meaning and task of this underlying 'Islam' been more comprehensively and sympathetically analysed in relation to the twentieth century than by Wilfred Cantwell Smith, *Islam in Modern History*, Princeton University Press, 1957.

shaikhs to provide creative, religious leadership for the modern generation. Their job was to preach and enjoin the ancient and revealed Shariah. Who were they, they asked, to 'find' solutions for the twentieth century? Could they presume to wrestle with the issues of the age or improve upon the solutions God Himself had 'found' and decreed? If asked whether the flux of time itself did not require a virile obedience, not improving but implementing God's solutions, they would not have recognized the question as significant. Their attitude must be understood with a lively sympathy. It has parallels in other faiths. What it fails to see is that revealed solutions are of necessity entrusted to co-operative minds. Such cannot contract out of their contemporary travail in the name of an eternal directive without betraying its eternal status. For the eternal relates to our temporal allegiance not in a passive acceptance but in an active obedience. The Divine demands and the sort of submission they await are the large issues underlying this question as to the temper and quality of a true Islam in this generation. It might readily be illustrated by a score of controversies and a spate of pamphlets in Cairo, Lahore, Baghdad or Damascus.

Inseparable from this debate is the understanding of the Quran and the form of its contemporary relevance. A Report of a Pakistan Government Commission on Marriage and Family Laws in that country, issued in June 1956, may be usefully cited here as a clear example of what is at stake. The Report observed:

So far as the Holy Book is concerned, the laws and injunctions promulgated therein deal mostly with basic principles and vital problems and consist of answers to the questions that arose while the Book was being revealed.

This view of the Quran's relevance leaves the field open for the application of the prophetic wisdom to 'situations and

54

problems not clearly envisaged in the Quran'.[1] Thus seen the Shariah is in no sense a closed entity, having a rigorous and literal finality.

A minority statement however follows the Report, made by Maulana Ihtishamul Haqq, a dissident member of the Commission. He roundly rejects these dangerous notions and insists that the Quran is literally the Divine wisdom. As it stands it is 'cognizant of every minor event of every period and every epoch from the beginning of time to its end'. He therefore ridicules the other members and their school and he taunts them by paraphrasing to their discomfort a Quranic verse (Surah v.8):

O ye Muslims of the period of revelation: Your religion has been perfected in regard to the circumstances of the period: but as regards future events it is imperfect and you can have it completed with the help of Commissions.[2]

These radically contrasted attitudes to Islamic loyalty belong in some measure to the whole course of twentieth-century Muslim discussion. Is the past wholly determinative of the present? Or is the present free to interpret and renew the past? Is today's generation to conform meticulously to the letter of the ancient word? Or is it required to apprehend the spirit of that word's demands as they relate to the manifold situations of the present day? Is such an appeal to 'spirit' destructive of the law's meaning? Are we right in supposing that anything circumstantial enters into the Quranic revelation? If not, how can we believe it really actual and historical? If so, and the circumstantial so manifestly differs from our circumstances, can our obedience be anything but creative?

What Islam is, then, as a matter both of definition and of temper, is the question that lies at the heart of Muslim

[1] *The Gazette of Pakistan*, no. S.1033, Karachi, June 20th 1956, p. 1199.　　　　[2] *Ibid.*, Karachi, August 30th 1956, p. 1565.

existence and fulfilment today. Debate as to the authentic Islam inevitably raises the issue of authority. Who is to give the authentic answer? Our critic in the mosque has made us feel the recent recession of 'shaikhly' leadership in life and letters. It has some features that resemble the emergence of 'lay' elements and forces in sixteenth- and seventeenth-century England, when politics, education and affairs, the arts and sciences, underwent a steady emancipation from ecclesiastical monopoly and the medieval universe of faith gave way to the modern multiverse of autonomies. Nineteenth- and twentieth-century Islam, at least in its most important territories, has experienced a great diversifying of its leadership. The old, unquestioned dominance of the 'ulama' or the *mujtahidun* in Sunni and Shiah Islam has suffered drastic revision.

It is illuminating to reflect on a comment of E. G. Browne, recalling the days of the Safavids in the heyday of Isfahan:

The power and position attained by these prelates tended to divert the ambitions of young men who possessed, or believed themselves to possess, the necessary intellectual qualifications, from poetry, belles lettres and other forms of mental activity, to theology, and from this tendency in part resulted the dearth of poets and abundance of divines under the Safavis. Those were spacious times for the turbaned classes and every poor, half starved student who frequented one or other of the numerous colleges founded, endowed and maintained by the piety of the Safavi Shahs who delighted to call themselves by such titles as 'Dog of the Threshold of the Immaculate Imams', or 'Promotor of the Church of the Twelve', dreamed no doubt of becoming at last a great Mujtahid wielding powers of life and death and accorded honors almost regal.[1]

Today the situation is remarkably reversed. It is Departments of Political Science that are crowded with aspirants

[1] E. G. Browne, *A Literary History of Persia*, vol. iv, 1928, p. 354.

after opportunity to govern. The exaltation of science explains the dearth of theologians (and poets) and the abundance of engineers and doctors. Graduates of venerable academies like Al-Azhar, Deoband, Al-Zaitunah and the Qairawin, find difficulty in securing a place in affairs or a status in society that adequately rewards the painstaking investment of their studies.

Very many more people then, and types of people, are claiming a share in the right to define Islam. Numerous pleas have been made for a revision, in Sunni Islam, of the qualification for *Ijtihad* (the technical name for endeavour leading to the formulation of legal opinions having validity in supplementing the Shariah). It is argued that meticulous acquaintance with the minutiae of Arabic grammar and *Tafsir* or Quranic exegesis, should give way, as necessary for *Ijtihad*, to established success in the commercial world and to proven experience in modern life.[1] The Report of the Commission on Marriage and Family Laws, earlier cited, itself directed numerous questions to a wide variety of Pakistani Muslims, inviting their views and comments on the matters at issue – all of them already involved in the ancient legislation. Should there be compulsory registration of marriages and divorces? Could there or should there be fixed ages for marriage? Should there be court provisos on the contraction of plural marriages? The questionnaire was calculated to be a kind of referendum in at least general application of the ancient principle of *Ijma* or consensus within which the whole community (whether under the stringent guidance of its officials or not) is determinative of Muslim 'truth', always provided that there is no repugnancy to the Quran and the Sunnah.

But the dissentient Ihtishamul Haqq at once quarrelled

[1] Ismail A. Faruki, *Ijma and the Gate of Ijtihad*, Karachi, 1954.

with this procedure and protested violently against its adoption. The grounds and terms of his protest make an illuminating comment on our quest for Islam. He wrote:

Reference to public opinion on matters of Shariah is intolerable on principle. As a matter of principle reference to public opinion on purely Shariah questions is trifling with Islamic Shariah and ridiculing the religion that can never be tolerated. Consulting every common man or even the leaders of sects which are by common consent excluded from the pale of Islam, on questions of Shariah which require considerable specialized experience and knowledge of religion, is to open a dangerous door to deliberate alterations in Islamic Shariah. When in medicine, engineering and law, which are mundane subjects based purely on human intellect, no sensible person can tolerate the opinion of the crowd, it is both against reason and religious sentiment to suggest consultation of the man in the street on the revealed Book of God and Divine laws.[1]

There could hardly be a plainer repudiation of the right of trespass on the preserves of the time-honoured custodians of Islam. The protest has added force by reason of the careful procedure of the questionnaire thus rejected. Its sponsors in no way suggested that the competence of this 'democracy' of referendum within *Ijma* was entire or even original. They merely strove after a definition of authoritative texts through popular comment. In its proposals the Report held with striking fidelity to the path of analogy, renouncing any pretensions to initiation and arguing for desirable changes on the ground that they were already analogically covered by existing provisions of the Quran. Thus, for example, marriages could legitimately be required to be registered because commercial transactions were required to be, and marriage is a much more serious 'transaction'. They pleaded for a minimum age for marriage on the ground that there

[1] *Op. cit.*, p. 1563.

were minimum ages already for the return of property to former wards. On this they said: 'The question of marriage may be decided on the same footing because the entrusting of the life of marrying parties to each other is an affair of greater importance than mere entrusting of property.'[1]

Yet for all this careful concern for validity by arguable analogy (for which there are honoured precedents), Ihtisha-mul Haqq had no stomach for the implications of the idea of popular reference. Yet it remains to be seen whether the times themselves will allow him and his type attitudes that resist change in order to perpetuate status. It has to be remembered that his dissentient opinion, though technically argued in these terms, was actually taken to buttress child-marriage and the many violations of women's rights in marriage that result from non-registration. The cause in which this particular action was fought may be taken as a further token of its obstinate tenacity.

Current Islamic writing, publication and debate are full of this kind of issue in a variety of forms. It lay behind the length of the debate on the Constitution of Pakistan. It has to do with the agitation and the suppression of the Muslim Brotherhood in Egypt. Let us be content to sum it up by quoting Ihtishamul Haqq. He states the issue squarely in his disapproval of all his fellow members of the Karachi Com-mission, on the ground that they 'had neither detailed knowledge of the Islamic teachings and injunctions' nor were 'versed in the interpretation and application of those laws'. As if forestalling similar arguments against himself, he went on:

There was no apparent harm in utilizing diverse talents but in the meetings of the Commission every member save myself assumed the position of an expert authority on Shariah and an

[1] *Ibid.*, p. 1209.

59

absolute Mujtahid. Hence they all remained one and united in contravention of the Holy Quran and the Sunnah and in ridiculing the Muslim jurisprudence and by calling their action as Ijma' (Consensus) in the Report they have debased the technical term of 'Shariah'.[1]

In the Maulana's view, appeal to popular consensus is a pretentious and inadmissible claim to *Ijtihad* on the part of every scholar so appealing. This to him spells chaos. But in resisting the dogmatism, as he regards it, of such consensus, he betrays the counter dogmatism of his own attitude, albeit based, as he sees it, on ancient and adequate criteria. Nor does he sense the relation of the new free 'dogmatism' of every Hasan, Salih and Ahmad (the Muslim version of Tom, Dick and Harry) to his own. He in fact represents what is a very familiar phenomenon. A mind on the defensive reproachfully identifies elsewhere the very temper by which it is itself falsely guided. To contravene what dogma says is valid seems to him the most outrageous absolutism leading straight to chaos. Yet it is precisely his own dogmatic absolutism that provokes the situation. For the only way of escape from it is to invoke new and contrary ideas with at least equal assurance. These are bound to seem outrageous to the old views they challenge.[2]

This single, but inclusive, example must suffice. Ihtishamul Haqq epitomizes for us no less effectively than Ahmad ibn Abdallah the issues that belong to the quest of Islam and that agitate Muslims today, be they conservers or renewers.

[1] *Ibid.*, p. 1562.
[2] The general line of the argument of the few preceding paragraphs and some of their language is taken, by permission of the Editor, from an article by the author in *Middle East Forum*, vol. xxxii, no. 9, Nov. 1957, pp. 15–17, and 33, 'The Tests of Islamicity'.

Each strives in his own light for the meaning of loyalty, its criteria and conditions.

'TO BE OR NOT TO BE'

Finally then our quest takes us, still in company with Muslim inquiry, to the ultimate question: How is Islam to be Islam? How is this submission of the Muslim, this actuality of the Divine Lordship, to be realized? The exhortations of the sermon are still in our ears: 'Purify your intention in word and deed . . . be warned against corrupting things . . . do not wrong your souls. . . . I enjoin upon you and upon myself, as servants of God, piety towards Him. Good success is to the God-fearing.' Muslim *minbars* ring with hortatory appeals. That is their principal purpose: to put the hearers in mind of the truth, to call them unto good. But how shall it be made actual? This is the question with which all questions end.

What does God-fearing mean in a technological age, in a Communist shadow, in a capitalist economy, in a scientific perplexity of power? Is the call to piety somehow efficacious just by being a call? It is significant for our answer that original Islam in the Prophet's hands found it imperative to link the faith with empire and the creed with government. Islam dates itself from the Hijrah, the time, not of its Prophet's birth or of its own birth as a thing preached, but its birthday as a polity, as a thing politically established.

By the community's emigration to Medina Muhammad secured what Mecca had stubbornly denied him, a foothold of authority that could be enlarged into a civil, and later an imperial, expression. That marriage of religion and state has ever since been elemental to Islamic genius and to Muslim history.

There are many in the modern Muslim world who seek and believe to find salvation in the same terms. With, beyond and sometimes even actually speaking in the mosque sermon must be the tongue, the arm, the will of the state.[1] Exhortation is a devotional category. But in the last analysis it speaks of an ideology recognized. Ideology fulfilled means, in some form or other, the action of the political order. Almost everywhere save in India, where the largest Muslim minority finds itself set in a multi-religious society with a secular statehood and no prospect of exclusively Islamic political norms, the political changes of the twentieth century have aided and enabled this philosophy. Islam has almost everywhere recovered the independent Muslim expression of its genius. With the departure of Western imperialisms, Muslims have recovered the political management of their own destinies. The strange aberration represented by nineteenth-century tutelage to non-Muslim power (or powers) is ended and with its termination has come, not only a great new sense of release and *élan*, but a deep debate as to the proper nature of the Islamic state that is once more blessedly feasible.

If the pursuit of this state has been, for example, the *raison d'être* of Pakistan, it has provoked there and elsewhere a sharp controversy as to just what it means and requires. The conservative view, represented by the *Jama'at-i-Islami*, with attitudes akin to those of the *Ikhwan-al-Muslimun* in the Arab world, is sure that the Islamic state should police

[1] A contemporary modern critic, Ali al-Wardy, a Baghdad author, in his *Wu'az al-Salatin* (1954), develops the thesis that the mosque pulpit has in general been subservient to state control. In the recent past, however, there have been several instances (notably in Egypt between the rise of the present regime and 1954 when the preachers came under direct state supervision) when the pulpit crossed swords with the will or policy of the state. But this may be taken rather as a measure of immediate issues between the point of view of certain preachers (especially within the Muslim Brotherhood) and that of the regime, than as evidence of any fundamental concept of an independent status for religious leadership *vis-à-vis* the political authority.

society in terms of the full Shariah and use its authority to enforce the revealed ideal and so demonstrate its benediction.

The contrary view is that the Shariah is ultimately a concept, a vision, a controlling aspiration, the definition of which calls for positive, creative thought, wise openness to mankind's accumulated experience both legal and political, and general adaptation of the institutions of democracy. There are many aspects of this fascinating discussion which we cannot here consider. But the emergent fact is that the mosque needs more than mosque, if Islam is to be fully Islam. Just as in pristine days the *minbar* was the *cathedra* of caliphal judgment and of political leadership, so now its exhortations need to be reinforced and sanctioned by the power of the prince or the president.

Just how far this political, legal actualization of ideology can go, is a question both Muslims and students of Islam must face by their own lights. Is the role of the state such that it can, or should, do more than hold the stage for the good life considered as ultimately dependent on wholly spiritual criteria? What is its own accountability and subservience to God? We will turn in Part 3 to some forms of Christian ministry in thought on this question and its religious implications. In the end, it must surely be recognized that there are realms of good, of truth, of God-relatedness, which necessarily transcend the competence of even the most ideal politics. The actuality of Islam in the sense that matters most – the sense to which all other meanings are subordinate – leads us back to the sanctuary.

While 'we have been thus musing' the *Salat* has happened, is happening. 'Happen' is the right word. For the ritual prayer is done, done with intention – the intention of worship. It is the sacramental posture and language of the submissive soul.

63

God is most great. God is most great. I bear witness that there is no god, except God: I bear witness that Muhammad is the apostle of God. God is most great. In the name of God, the merciful Lord of mercy. Praise be to God, the Lord of the worlds, the merciful Lord of mercy. Sovereign of the day of judgment. Thee alone it is we worship: Thee alone we implore to help. Guide us in the straight path, the path of those unto whom Thou art gracious, who are not the in-currers of Thy anger, nor wanderers in error. God is most great, God is most great. . . . I bear witness that Muhammad is the Apostle of God. . . . May God send down blessing upon him and preserve him in peace. Peace rest upon you (all) and the mercy of God.

The worshippers, who with intention have completed their *Raka'at*, are unified on the *Qiblah*, or Meccan pole of prayer behind the Imam. On the *Qiblah* our quest comes to its term. The *mihrab* in the mosque indicates the direction of the Great Mosque in Mecca, in whose precincts Muhammad first proclaimed the sinful folly of idolatry and the sole worship of God. On that radius every mosque is constructed. This unifying gesture of facing Mecca at prayer proclaims and recognizes the centrality of the Quranic revelation. It is both a geographical expression of allegiance and a sacrament of its theological content. An exercise in devotion, it symbol-izes commitment to a set of doctrines and ideological demands, which are meant to be to the Muslim's life what the *Qiblah* is to his prayers.

While the *mihrab* in this way determines the spiritual axis of the mosque and its people, the faith claims to determine the axis of their whole existence. To miss or ignore the *Qiblah* would be to disqualify the prayer. Similarly political constitutions are to be tested by the principle of non-repug-nancy to the Quran (to borrow one of the phrases most conspicuous in the long constitutional debates in Pakistan

from 1948 to 1956). The documents of the faith provide the
proper orientation for the political instrument of the nation's
government. In like manner in the realms of thought and
dogma, what repugnancy is in constitutions, *kufr* or unbelief is in intellectual systems. The valid, with its explicit
veto on the invalid, is ideally as potent and as definitive in
every realm as the *Qiblah* is in the ritual of devotion. As a
criterion then we may take it here as both a parable and a
symbol, signifying the decision of Muslims for Islam. The
quest of historic Islam is for its own distinctive meaning in
realization. To have reached that definition means that the
Christian student is also at the end of his immediate venture
in knowledge. But that end, like the definition itself, is
really a new beginning – a beginning in informed, imaginative relationship. The congregated worshippers make their
departure, retake their sandals and stream out into the
business of their lives. They go out from the *Qiblah* tangible
into the *Qiblah* intangible, into the 'to be or not to be' of
their submission.

The Christian, too, resumes his way. If his knowledge has
deepened, so also has his responsibility. In the light of the
one, what is he to do with the other?

PART 2

Conditions of Inter-Religion

>>> ✧ <<<

COMMON DENOMINATORS OF CIRCUMSTANCE

OFTEN in a work of fiction the reader finds on a fly-leaf a protective disclaimer from the author, assuring him that none of the characters in the story bear any relation to living persons. Not being about fictitious things this book prefers the note prefacing a recent work on law and its infractions which ran:

All the characters in this book are real persons, who are hereby invited to give it invaluable publicity by issuing writs for libel.

Or if such lust for litigation more befits the lawyer than the student, let us say that our concerns are very much in and with the living world of day-to-day people. All the characters personal and representative, whom we have already encountered, are indeed real persons, as we are who seek and read.

It is as such that we arrive at our further theme of inter-religion. Because we are all immersed in living situations to which our faiths relate and are not academic abstractions with no duties of decision and of destiny, we are compelled to ask ourselves where we go from the point at which our first venture ended when we turned the page.

The answer of the academician, quite simply, is that we go no further. Study is a self-sufficient end. To investigate, to clarify, to expound, but not to relate or mediate – these are the duties of pure scholarship. Perhaps so: though there are few sciences that exist only to be pure. The point of their pure form, as in mathematics, geometry, physics, is that applied forms may be served and guided. Religion, by definition, can never be abstraction and, therefore, theology can never be only pure, abstract, aloof and theoretical. Faith is conviction and commitment. God, its theme and goal, is never an academic topic – a blasphemous, and indeed also a ludicrous impossibility. He that comes to God must believe that He is. Any study of Islam that is content only to discourse and to discuss is *ipso facto* a contradiction of Islam. Nobody is validly studying what he begins by denying. Pundits have found this truth hard to recognize. By all means let us investigate Islam. But do not let us suppose that we are therein exempted from having to do with God.

Those sandals, then, and the totality of the system within which they are doffed at the gate, are bigger than they seem. But when we attempt to do more than study them, a perplexing perspective opens up before us. Can there conceivably be such a thing as inter-religion? Are not the historic systems of belief and worship closed circuits of adherence and allegiance? Are they not properly circumscribed by tokens of communal belonging, ceremonies of initiation and obligation and a natural possessiveness over their adherents? Do not even those who pride themselves on an easy toleration of others, based on a belief in the relative truth of all, develop, like Hinduism, a quite sharp intolerance of those that claim the ultimate truth of one? Thus ideas of universal hospitality to which some incline, contain within themselves seeds of an exclusiveness as complete as that asserted by the plainly intolerant.

In any event, it will be said, it is precisely in their separateness that great religions find their force. A syncretism that proposes to conflate or somehow reconceive them, fails to do justice either to their content or to the sense of them that sustains their disciples. Religions compared are, in some sense, religions evaporated. Being what you are – Buddhist, Hindu, Muslim – is, in our day and throughout the centuries, so much a part of a corresponding sense of what you are not. Loyalty belongs, it would seem, only to wholeness of self-identity.

In these and many other considerations which it is not the place to discuss here, it is not difficult to discern the dimensions of our problem. If we needed sympathy and a certain transcendence of ourselves in order to understand Islam, we need those capacities deepened if we are to move further into communication in transactions of thought and word. What, it will be asked, is the inter-religion we mean?

Clearly there is in our time a far-reaching *fact* of inter-religion in the simple circumstance we may describe as inter-life. Thoughts in the mosque have shown as much. No argument, only a little imagination, is necessary to sustain the truth of man's involvement with man and thus religion's involvement with religion.

The mutual openness in large measure of the cultures within the one world needs no emphasis. Humanity has always been a somewhat gregarious affair. But man's not living, and not dying, unto himself was formerly on a local and restricted scale. Within the seclusions of geography, of culture, of economy, of ignorance, man's need of his neighbour and his peril from him were circumscribed. Today, there are no secure limits to the menacing range of our precariousness and our involvement with forces in the control of others. The demure drawing-rooms of Jane Austen's novels overheard many an apprehensive, if still becoming, conversation, as the fabric of personal hopes and envies, fears and enmities, was woven into destiny, by a little coterie

69

of fellow-weavers. But inside their protective walls came no hint of intrusive forces, whether from Waterloo or Peterloo. It was a world bounded by a charmed circle of oblivion. Today that drawing-room, where one made another's fate, dismayed his hopes or tortured his fears, has become the unbounded world, with neither charm nor seclusion, but only exposure and inescapable uncertainty.

Man in this generation lives under the shadow of his nuclear power and the unreconciled competition of his ideological divisions. The common features of our situation are the most compulsive and the most intractable. Second only to the scientific and political factors themselves is the incredible speed with which they revolutionize our situation.

It is only two short decades since Islam was related to Christianity within the framework of circumstances created by the Pax Britannica and the structure of western imperialism. In that incredibly brief period the European nations of that imperialism have themselves passed under a far more desperate form of dependence upon external power, which, though it may be sincerely constituted as an alliance, has none of the prospects of termination which two decades ago, were opening into fulfilment for their erstwhile dependants in Asia and the Middle East. Europe in the nuclear age has undergone an awesome reversion of status, in terms of the actualities of power and survival. The newly self-responsible nations find their political destinies in their own hands and yet, in the truest sense, out of their hands and in other people's arms – unless by dint of neutralism their wits can make a precarious security out of a bargainer's market.

But the immediate point is that the realities of the evolving scene make vast new common denominators of circumstance for the religious faiths of the world. Man has never had so much so desperately and so urgently in common, than the current elusiveness of peace in the political and ideological realms of the world's life, upon which all other realms turn in the end for survival. It is doubtless true that religions and cultures react much more in terms of the past they inherit than of the future they face. Religious expression is among the most tenacious and conservative of human phenomena. Yet the pressure of contemporary realities may leave the conservative with nothing to conserve unless he can creatively transcend a mere assertive conservatism.

There is no place here to analyse the various forms of theological reaction in Islam to these realities, nor to narrate even in broad detail the main course of the twentieth-century impact – the postponements of Arab nationalism; its still unresolved dilemmas; the parallel emergence of Israeli statehood, with all its consequences for Arab feeling and fortunes; the great experiment of Pakistani Islamic statehood; the novel and exacting situation of Indian Muslims; the uncertain story of Indonesian Islam in its vast territories; the slow evolution of the millions of Negro Islam in Africa; the far-reaching implications of Marxian and Khruschevian Communism in the wide frontier territories beside the iron curtain and in the continental hinterland behind those Soviet borders.

In all these national and political developments, and part of the passion, pride and perplexity they generate, are massive changes in the economic structure and the social order. There are immense new oil revenues, oddly distributed geographically, but reshaping whole economies and their dependent societies. Most other economies in the Muslim areas, not being so endowed, seek large-scale capital development. This in turn has brought into being a new kind of inter-involvement of countries and continents, in which, paradoxically, political and ideological cleavage makes for

71

intensifying competition. Behind this necessity for capital and the context of ideological struggle in which it proceeds, is the ever-growing pressure of increasing populations upon available resources. The pace, too, of our contemporary changes is manifestly self-accelerating. There are the answers we fail to find now, the questions we cannot control to-morrow. Our world is big with the unpredictable. Men are afraid because they do not know what to think.

This bigness in the world of our time, in the midst of its visible shrinkage, is a bigness that grows with the very contraction of its physical distances. In this context the life of religious beliefs and practice proceeds. While being exposed the more to each other through the concentration of fears, the religions of the world are tested by the magnitude of their new setting. Unprecedented times make new and com-pelling reasons for mutual relation. Modern man is required by his very modernity to extend his readiness for common thinking and depending into areas formerly insulated in confident seclusion or immune from the perplexities of disruption.

Whatever, then, may or should be the shape of relations between religions, consciously undertaken and pursued, they are in fact in a state of real actual co-existence to a degree never true hitherto. It is not argued that common predica-ments necessarily bring them together. They may aggravate rather than facilitate their mutual life. But there can be no mistaking the increasing extent to which that life *is*, materi-ally and physically, mutual.

It may be that the situation makes, in some sense, for an increasing competition between the systems of faith. It is notable, for example, that in the recent past strenuous efforts have been made by both Buddhism and Islam to commend themselves far outside their familiar territories as the proper religions for the western world. Such an enterprise is based upon the alleged failure of Christianity to discipline and guide Western civilization – a failure which accounts, it is said, for the now universal menace of Western technology and nuclear power. Those two religions have thus made the general political and external search for security an occasion for strong and assertive religious competitiveness with the stakes laid in their claim to greater ideological adequacy both to West and East. These religions believe that they have what it takes and their very certainties are intertwined with their conviction of inadequacy elsewhere.

Whatever may be thought of these arguments, at least it is clear that religious systems are compelled by events to address themselves to the same problems, whereas in former centuries and in their erstwhile isolations of distance they scarcely knew each other's worlds. Thus even if the consequence of the new setting be a sharpened competition, the competing claims have to be related to the same general set of facts. Inter-religion, in that sense, is proved by the seemingly contradictory fact of counter-religion.

Ultimately, however, the latter only becomes possible because that to which religions relate is the common denominator of human nature. Debating adequacy, though it be in competitive and thus divisive terms, implies that there is a common field of religious purpose, if only in the question: adequate to what? We need not accept any merely functional idea of faith to agree that the answer presupposes a single human context, in which superiority is to be displayed. This was always so. But contemporary conditions have made it plain and inescapable.

'MEN OF LIKE PASSIONS'

The second great fact of inter-religion, therefore, is the

universal abiding fact of human nature, within the common obligation to present and universal conditions of life. There is inter-religion in the fundamental sense that mankind is one in its elemental needs, yearnings, wistfulness and fear. Religions, across all their disparities, are about the same thing and have to do with the same world, with the heart of man and the finitude of life. There is no occasion to argue this fact. The one denominator of the human situation, it is true, may well make all the while for counter-religion. For there are categorically divided notions as to what humanity is all about and what are its feasible attitudes. But again, the very possibility of controversies amid religions on these themes means that their elemental subject matter is one and the same. There might be risk in emphasizing the obvious, were it not for the fact that the obvious is often the neglected.

The whole matter can be illustrated by the commonness in antipathy, the like amid the contrary, evident in the realm of Islam and Christianity. By their basic commitment to belief in the significance of the world, the oneness and personality of God, the fact of revelation and the moral accountability of man in and beyond this life, these two faiths have close affinities, not shared in the relations of either with the religions of further Asia. Since even with these last a wide realm of commonness in the fact of man is always present, the inter-quality of these two in their understanding of man is deeper still.

Islam and Christianity deal fundamentally with the same things and to a significant extent deal with them in the same way. The distinctiveness that lies beyond the commonness is serious and inclusive, and reaches back inevitably to qualify what is shared. The Christian presence in witness has to do critically and gloriously with this distinctiveness. But only on the ground-fact of things in common. Prophecy, worship, prayer, mercy, law, scriptures, patriarchs, God's signs in nature, creation and sin – all these are religious categories having to do with the Divine relation to the human situation.

The extent of common Biblical and Quranic terms and phrases serves to confirm the point. The two final Surahs of the Quran, known as the *Muawidhdhatan*,[1] or 'the two refuge seekers' belong, at least potentially, with the Biblical: 'God is our refuge and strength', and with Christian hymnology: 'Other refuge have I none'. Some aspects of the fears from which refuge is sought there – jinns and whispers of men – find no parallel in the Biblical refuge and could never have inspired Charles Wesley's lines. Yet there is the underlying conviction that – to quote another parallel phrase – 'Our sufficiency is of God' (cf. Surah viii.63 et al.).

God is, moreover, *Al-Samad*, as Surah cxii proclaims. The meaning of the word has deep kinship with the 'I AM' of Ex. 3.14. God has all resources in Himself, so that He sustains all and is sustained by none. Thus He is the resort of all. Yet the all-resourceful God is 'near in His majesty'. That Muslim phrase echoes the cry of the Biblical prophet that God has humbled Himself to behold the things that are in heaven and earth. Such close affinities of thought, language and religious posture, though never far from radical divergencies, are too wide and real to be disregarded. They mean a significant agreement about man's status before God.

---

[1] These two Surahs run: 'In the name of the merciful Lord of mercy. Say: I seek refuge with the Lord of the dawn from the evil in creation, from the evil of the brooding darkness, from the evil of conjuring witches, from the evil envying of the envious. In the Name of the merciful Lord of mercy. Say: I seek refuge with the Lord of men, with the God of men, from the evil of furtive, whispering schemers that whisper in the hearts of men, from jinns and men.' The rhymes of these verses defy translation without sacrifice of meaning, but the reader should bear in mind the influence they have in the original.

Our human situation does yet more for the inter-penetration of our two faiths. It involves both, indeed all, faiths in similar frailties and compromise. While theologians, with justice, discriminate and distinguish, the sinners and the saints, the ordinary in their belonging and the extra-ordinary, tend to defy the distinctions in loosely comparable situations of delinquency or attainment. Doubtless neither are measured, as between faiths, by the same standards or criteria. But they recur with discernible similarities. Human nature to that extent makes religions kin. The menace of pride and complacence, of hypocrisy and lip-service, of unworthiness in allegiance and corruption in discipleship, casts shadows over all creeds. It is useless to attempt comparison quantitatively of the moral forms of religious failure.

The universal reach of such phenomena across the frontiers of theologies and creeds warrants no loose or easy supposition that the latter are indistinguishable. Unworthiness within systems is diversely identified, reproached or condoned, and there is certainly wide disparity in the capacity to feel, and much more to retrieve, such inward evils. But it can hardly be denied that the far reach of comparable unworthiness in life is another aspect of the essential untidiness of reality, defying the neat contrasts of formal theologies and abstract claims.

There is inter-religion in the capacity of both the Muslim Harun al-Rashid and the Christian Henry VIII to be at once both zealously pious and brutally venal. Hypocrites, likewise, differ from religion to religion. But the hypocrisy is the same. Traders in superstition and the gullible whom they exploit have a way of looking alike whether you are reading the *Canterbury Tales* or the *Arabian Nights*. The knaves are diverse, but the knavery is one. If Christianity has had rulers for whom cities were worth masses, Islam has known caliphs for whom they were worth prostrations. Or go outside church and mosque a moment and reflect on the steady practice of world deception revealed in the letters of Cicero. None can deny when he returns to Christian or Muslim precincts that there are Ciceros in both – men whose front to the world is lauded and admired, who even become their culture's eager pride, whose inward soul is full nevertheless of despicableness and deceit.

This state of affairs, incidentally, raises serious questions for an imperfect concept of 'conversion'. Too often the latter tends to be thought of as necessarily turning on a communal transference of allegiance or on a mere credal affirmation. Wherever the issues in man's inward remaking are underestimated, we can expect that human nature will surely defy or defeat the surface changes. Bishop Stephen Neill has well observed how persistent through the generations are the recurrent attitudes with which conversion was supposed to have effectively dealt.

On a deeper level than conduct and in the end more menacing is the persistent underground of non-Christian structures and patterns of thought. . . . They persist in all of us, racially as well as individually. . . . This explains the distressing emergence in the third and fourth generations of Christians of old evil practices such as one would imagine to have long since disappeared from the Christian consciousness. . . . This inner schism cannot be dealt with by the multiplication of Christian ceremonies and practices. All outward and indeed inward Christian life is built on an insecure foundation until the inner schism is radically healed.[1]

The transformation of the person needs to be thought of in other dimensions than those of the person alone. The implications of this situation for the whole theology of con-

[1] Stephen C. Neill, *The Unfinished Task*, London, Edinburgh House Press, 1957, pp. 117–118.

version demand that we think not only of what may be called trans-religious, but of inter-religious, transformation. Men need a spiritual revolution that not only goes across the frontiers but penetrates the hinterlands. To be a Muslim (or Hindu or Buddhist) is to be part of a total culture and to be set in a corporate context of personality. The redemption of human nature likewise cannot finally be complete in wholly individual terms. The familiar and characteristically Christian truth is that being 'in Christ' involves a personal decisiveness. But we have traditionally interpreted being 'in Christ' in terms insufficiently social and corporate.

Be these fascinating conjectures as they may, the present concern of the argument is clear. Human nature, in its erring and repairing, makes for an inter-religious situation. Salvation in Christ occurs in the midst of a personal history and positively bears on an inescapable past. Regeneration has to do with what a man has been, and remains, as well as with what he becomes. 'The old and the new' involved in Christian conversion are not merely an earlier and a later creed. The old man it is who is being remade in the new: the new man he who newly perpetuates the old. Conversion must be seen within the continuum of the human person. The old is not simply a character that passes, but the ground of new character that persists. We must avoid the confusion of thought which takes the new for the abolition of the old, rather than its transformation. 'Thou art Simon . . . thou shalt be . . . Peter' (John 2.42).

Thus, conversion itself, so often regarded as the focal point of otherness between any two religions, is an event within a continuity that positively involves both. This fact, arising from the commonness of human nature, is only a further confirmation of our general point. Despite the obvious irritants of communal transference in all the present emotional and political circumstances, the only reasons that validly bring a Muslim into Christ belong essentially to the same human situation under God with which it is the business of Islam to deal. The two continue to be relevant to each other, even when obscuring or vociferous attitudes deny it.

The same conclusion faces us if we come upon the matter from the other side and attend to saintliness rather than wrongdoing as a phenomenon between religions. Again the fact gives no excuse for easy conclusions that all religions are alike. Nor is it feasible or desirable to attempt comparative statistics of genuine piety. What is certain is that there are deep elements of mystery and awe about this theme. Belief in the Christian criteria and conditions of the good life, and recognition of movements of the Spirit elsewhere, must be held together. Al-Ghazali was in some areas of his writing sharply contra-Christian. But there is no doubt that his experience of despair and wandering, of assurance and of a 'rescuer', are in the realm of spiritual kinship with the meanings of Christ. His sense of the labyrinth of human temptations and of the depths of the cry of man for a truly clean heart have an undeniable place with the masters of Christian ascetic theology. There are other masters of the Spirit in the two faiths, who belong in part together, in inward significance if not in outward community.

We might take, almost at random, this extract from a familiar Prayer Manual of the well-known Tijani Order of Sufis, founded in the late eighteenth century by Abu-l-Abbas Ahmad al-Tijani, who died in the year of the battle of Waterloo. Fez in Morocco and Tlemcen in Western Algeria were his main centres. The depth and urgency of entreaty in this passage find many echoes elsewhere in this rich literature of Muslim devotion. Its language might well be baptized into Christian use.

79

O my God, I have no thought of Thee, save what is beautiful: I see in Thee nought but graciousness. To me Thy goodness is all-embracing. Thy works in my sight are perfect. Thy mercy is to me ever reliable: Thy righteousness a forgiving righteousness, Thy bountifulness towards me constant and perpetual, Thy benefits towards me unremitting. Thou hast obviated my fears and fulfilled my hopes, hast realized my desires and befriended me in my travels, restored me in my sicknesses, healed my diseases and dealt kindly with my up-heavals and my home making.

Or these petitions from a Shiah manual of Prayers for the sacred month of Ramadan, with their haunting but un-explained identity of thought with the Magnificat of the New Testament:

Praise be to God who has no competitor to equal Him, nor peer to compare with Him, nor helper to aid Him. With His might He subdues the mighty and by His greatness the great are humbled. Whatever He wills by His power He attains. Praise be to God Who hearkens unto me when I call upon Him, Who covers my unworthiness when I have been rebellious against Him and magnifies His grace upon me. . . . I will sing unto His praise and make mention of Him in thanksgiving. Praise be to God, Whose veil is never rent (here a contrasted thought: cf. Mark 15.38), Whose door is never barred, Who repels none that seek Him nor disappoints their hope. Praise be to God, Who preserves those that fear Him, lifts up those who are despised and sets down the arrogant.

Kinships of saintliness and of disciplined asceticism characterize mystics and mysticism. These are well known for their relative detachment from canons of orthodoxy and for the way in which they are apt to become, doctrinally, a law unto themselves. In some quarters suspicion of mysticism as holding too loosely to dogma is held to justify a will to discount it as unrepresentative. At least it is suggested that the similarities of mystics are one thing, the contrasts of dogmatic systems quite another. Yet it is impossible to disqualify Islamic Sufism and Christian mysticism from being Islamic and Christian, whatever the tensions with orthodox custodians. The whole genius of mysticism remains a moving testimony to common features of self-abnegation, penitence, absorption, ecstasy and contemplation, which reinforce the truth of mutuality through divergence. This inter-religious significance of mystical patterns and attainment cannot be dismissed as heterodox. Nor can it be denied without such opinion being further evidence of the inability of religions to escape from what is common to religion.

But the case for comparable sanctity in personal life need not turn exclusively upon Sufis and their Christian counterparts. In the end, perhaps, too much mystery attaches to Meister Eckhart and Al-Hallaj. The ordinary man of prayer may be pardoned for supposing that Shams-ud-Din and St John of the Cross are souls apart. There remains, however, a vast realm of religious existence – struggles with conscience (albeit differently ordered); fidelity under temptation; quiet patience under adversity; the tranquillity of reliance upon God in sorrow – what Islam calls *itmi'nan* and Christianity 'the quiet mind' – as these become evident in the daily life of simple folk. 'O Lord in Thee have I trusted' is the closing confession of the *Te Deum Laudamus*. It is also one of the most frequent and characteristic phrases of Muslim devotion. What such self-entrustment unto God means in the articulate experience of Muslim and Christian has qualitative differences that should be recognized, in so far as they are accessible. But it is plain that there is, religiously, a real attitude in common, as in many another theme of man's perpetual finitude and creaturehood under God.

The foregoing has not solved any final questions. It has only indicated certain general facts that justify the term

F

'inter-religion' as a proper description of what our human situation discloses, as both the twentieth century and essential man have shaped it. One remaining consideration takes us back briefly to the realm of the political.

MEN'S FAITHS AND THEIR NATIONALISM

Islam and Christianity belong to an inter-religious situation, not only on account of the common perplexities of the age and the constant nature of man whatever the age, but also by reason of the fact that they share, though seldom in equal numerical proportion, the onus of national solidarity. There are minority Christian communities in the major Muslim states, except Arabia itself and North Africa. In Egypt, Syria, Jordan, Iraq and the Lebanon there are Coptic, Orthodox, Armenian, Syriac and other Christian Churches whose ancestry antedates Islam by several centuries. In all but the last these minorities are never more, often much less, than one eighth of the whole population.[1]

One of the deep questions of the Arab national movement is whether its ethos is Islamic in the sense that the non-Muslim Arab is at best a minor partner, at worst a tolerated inferior, or whether the religious allegiance of the majority serves an Arabism that transcends Islam. What is the spirit of the near identity which must exist between Arabism and Islam? The question is obviously vital for the non-Muslim elements. Not that they have any option. The die is certainly cast for Arab solidarity and the only Arab security is with

[1] The 1946 census, which was the last to be taken in Lebanon, gave 461,827 Muslims (244,307 being Sunnis and 217,520 Shiahs), 77,023 Druses and 599,266 Christians of whom 337,734 were Maronites, 113,197 Greek Orthodox, 61,600 Armenian Gregorian and 10,783 Protestant. The Christian-Muslim ratio is now very much closer, though what it precisely is remains a matter of conjecture and sharp political controversy.

82

and from Islam. But the ramifications of the issue are very far-reaching, in education, law, society and culture. The situation is an exacting occasion of inter-religion – the more so because it is inescapable. It makes demands upon the spirit and practice of each faith and goes far below the surface of events.

In the southern Sudan, in Nigeria and elsewhere, there are inter-religious situations of a different sort, since the Christianity is mainly recent (though not lacking ancient precedents in Africa). It is ex-pagan and illiterate. The integration of a single country out of diverse, and culturally competing, elements is surely, among other things, a problem 'between religions'. In some areas in West Africa there is a free social intermingling and an attitude of easy co-existence.[1]

But elsewhere consciousness of difference, of majority Muslim strength, of minority Christian weakness, is pointed and keen. In other parts of Negro Africa, west, east and central, there is a slow permeation of paganism by both faiths, with differing forms of impact and process. The whole story is only very sketchily documented and analysis is difficult. How can one be content only to hint at a continent? What vast dimension belongs to inter-religion in Negro Africa, and like everything African it is big with possibility.

Pakistan, likewise, and Indonesia have small Christian minorities, while that in Malaya, smaller still, is also racially distinctive, being almost wholly non-Malay.[2] Ethiopia, always

---

[1] The writer was invited, for example, to comment, in a mixed school of Muslims and Christians in Freetown, Sierra Leone, on the practice of inviting Muslim friends to act as godparents in Christian baptism. It was evidently quite a familiar thing.

See *The Muslim World*, vol. xlviii, 3, July 1958, pp. 237–247, 'West African Catechism'.

[2] Latest available figures put the Muslim proportion in the total population of Pakistan at 86.9%, with Hindus 13% and Christians

a Christian nation, except for interludes of Muslim conquest, has a Muslim minority of perhaps two fifths or more. Here the Arab problem of inter-religion exists in reverse direction. Increasing political self-awareness in the Muslim communities and the adjacent issue of independence for Italian Somaliland complicate the problem within Ethiopia. In India both the forty or so million Muslims and the small Christian groups have at least in common the status of minorities over against Hinduism. All these are familiar facts deserving careful analysis, not bald mention.

This pattern of nationalism is one of the marks which the retreating West has left upon Asia. As compared with caliphal empires, there is no doubt that it sharpens the inter-religious situation. In the older, larger unities, Islam was of course the dominant religious principle of cohesion and in imperial form its dominance was universal. Within the nation states it still preponderates. But these, in their territorial units, have introduced a new principle of cohesion in nationality, which partially at least in emotion, and totally in law, separates Muslims within from Muslims without and contrariwise unites non-Muslims and Muslims within. The pan-Islamic idea in some vague sense, particularly inside the United Nations, aims to retain the old universal reach of the single household. But the realities of political existence are plainly and, it would seem, irreversibly national.[1]

This fact of nationality alters as it were the horizontal

0.7%. There are some three million Christians in a population (1948) of around seventy-eight million in Indonesia. Christians in Malaya numbered 133,605 in 1948 in a population numbering nearly five million in 1947 and estimated now at over six million.

[1] Iqbal's idea that such nationalism was only a temporary stage in the dislodgment of the west from Asia, and one that would give way to Islamic empire once its negative purpose was fulfilled seems entirely belied by events. See Muhammad Iqbal, *Lectures on a Reconstruction of Religious Thought in Islam*, Lahore, 1931.

84

strata of religions and communities across the caliphal dominion and turns them into vertical divisions down the unity of Islam, giving an external unity to different religious elements within a single state. The intense economic, legal and social issues arising within such new statehood, coupled with constitutional definition, judicial reform and ideological theory, clearly make for greater and more exacting involvement of differing religions with each other. The exhilaration of the situation may lead the dominant religion into fresh postures of self-sufficiency; or its complexity may induce in some quarters a sober realism. But either event – or others the reader may conjecture – means that inter-religion is very much a fact, whatever form it takes.

Such, then, factually, are the conditions of inter-religion today. But in another sense of the word 'conditions', what ought to be the shape of mutual relation between faiths? Having the world, man and society somehow in common, on what principles should they guide their intercourse? What should be their attitudes and objectives in respect of each other? From inter-religion as one of the facts of our existence, we turn to think of it as a conscious ordering of relationship.

Clearly the answers can only come from within each faith for itself. Only Muslims can determine the Islamic duty *vis-à-vis* Christians. The aim of what follows is to consider the shape of Christian duty *vis-à-vis* Muslims, in the light both of the foregoing facts of common time, humanity and society, and of the inner self-awareness of Christian faith. Our reflections will be tested by reference to the significance of the threefold temptations of Christ as they bear upon Christianity's encounter with non-Christianity.

'HER WAYS ARE WAYS OF GENTLENESS'

All truly Christian relationships begin and continue in

85

humility. We are creatures of a Gospel which proclaims the amazing wonder of the self-humiliation of the Lord of all. No one can be in true trusteeship of the good news of Bethlehem and serve his trust with arrogance. None can truly preach the Gospel of the Cross, unless he has first accepted the lowly estate where the Cross finds him. The good news has to be made known in the temper that matches its events. There is a beautiful sense of this reciprocity, between the events and the service of them, in the Magnificat, or Song of Mary. 'My soul doth magnify the Lord. . . . He hath regarded the lowliness of His handmaiden.' The recognition of the Divine greatness, the Christian *Takbir*,[1] springs from the sense of the Divine condescension. The initiative of God fulfils itself in a lowly partnership with the earthly instrument. 'He hath regarded . . . recognized, prized, esteemed, stooped to, our low estate.' Mary's words interpret the inner meaning of the Incarnation in an act of worship that greets and accepts the vocation it requires. God calls us into service, deigns to employ our lowly instrumentality, because He treasures the fellowship of our mortality. So He initiates His Divine forgiveness as a seeking and a saving of the world.

This recognition in the very Gospel itself of the worth of man to God means a lowliness in God's very greatness. The nature of His omnipotence is such as we learn at the Manger and the Cross. The secret of our dignity under grace is one with the compulsion to humility. The same truth faces us when we reflect upon the indwelling of the Holy Spirit.

The texture of our truest thoughts about God must be woven out of earthly stuff, however heavenly the pattern of divine

[1] The term indicating the adoring cry: *Allahu Akbar* — 'God is most great' which is the most characteristic word in all Muslim devotion.

grace shown by it. The whisper of the Spirit must come to *our* ears, the impulse of the Spirit must fall upon *our* minds that have always to recognize and interpret the divine event that has befallen us. We shall be taught humility and saved from fanaticism, if we realize more clearly this *kenosis* of the Spirit.[1]

The amazing wonder that a man can be the temple of the Holy Spirit is an infinitely humbling thing. For in the fact of its being so is the mystery of the patient condescension of God. It is little wonder that Dr Wheeler Robinson goes on to cite the remarkable words of old Horace Bushnell:

The Spirit 'has His Gethsemane within us . . . if the sacrifices of the much enduring, agonizing Spirit were acted before the senses in the manner of the incarnate life of Jesus, He would seem to make the world itself a kind of Calvary from age to age'.[2]

What room then for aught save humility in a situation at once so involved in the lowliness of God in Christ by the Spirit? Outside a comparable lowliness the Christian has no valid status. His being in reconciliation and in ministry hinges upon the self-giving of God. All his relationships must be in the truth of his own inner Christian existence.

This obligation to humility would be what it is irrespective of any external aspects of Christian duty. Relationships in pride are not relationships in Christ. But the need for the recognition of this truth is reinforced by many external considerations belonging to the world around us. The whole realm of man's worship is, quite evidently, permeated with mystery. Awe, as at the arrest of Moses by the burning bush, is our proper attitude. He who deals with men's faiths, it is

---

[1] H. Wheeler Robinson, *Redemption and Revelation*, Nisbet, London, 1942, pp. 294–295. The whole passage on 'The Kenosis of the Spirit' is a moving statement of a great, but often forgotten truth.   [2] Quoted from *ibid.*, p. 293.

said, should know that he moves amid their yearnings. Interfaith situations have suffered from improper simplifications of their issues.

Nor is this argued merely on a tactical score. It is true that he who would persuade and inform does not well to begin by repelling. What communication involves can never be out of place in the service of a Gospel which is itself the communication of God. Christian theology is safest when it is most concerned, not to be safe, but to be articulate. The impulse to reverence, tactfulness, tenderness, care, sensitivity – in a word – to humility, in the presence of inter-religious complexity is much more than simply right tactics. In all that has to do with finitude and with eternity, it is well to remember the plea of Oliver Cromwell: 'For God's sake, I pray you, bethink you, you may be mistaken.' If we aspire to be vehicles among men of God's Holy Spirit, had we not better dwell in that consciously low estate, in that humility of mind, for which alone He has regard?

Within this authority of humility, our other need in the Christian relation with Islam is for fulness and openness. There must be no conspiracies of silence, no partialities of convenience. Frankness has to be honestly at work in two directions – recognition and crisis. It must base itself, that is, upon the deepest and fullest meanings of Islam. It must be ready to enter positively into a rich participation in the inclusive potential reach of Muslim thought and experience. There is no validity in a relationship that aims only to minimize or to discredit.

But on the other hand, the Christian must speak out of the deepest and fullest meanings of Christ. These bring crisis and decision into every context. It is necessary, therefore, to brace and school ourselves for the creative trust of what is distinctive. For a relationship that tranquillizes all issues is no more valid than the one which aggravates all contrasts. Honesty in humility has duties in both directions which in the end will be found to belong together. The surest way to do the fullest justice to Christianity as a Gospel is to take the fullest measures of Islam as law.

Yet this is precisely what so often the Christian has failed to do. The Church has tended to over-simplify its thoughts on Islam. It is liable to assume that a static picture of decades or even centuries ago is still valid. Certain unhappy features – fatalism, hostility, polygamy, stagnancy – are too easily thought of as being characteristically Muslim. 'Islam reformed is Islam no longer' we were assured by Lord Cromer.[1] And though the dictum was, and is, fatuous, we are prone to accept it unchallenged. So the Church appears sometimes almost in league with Muslim unworthiness, discounting items of worthy change as unreal or unrepresentative, or imputing them wholly to external factors. Apart from possibly failing in this regard to 'rejoice with the truth', as St Paul puts it in his song of praise to love, the Church fails also to keep her relationships abreast of historical facts.

The Christian attitudes to Islam must be sensitive especially to those areas of Islamic development in law or culture that bring it into closer approximation to Christian ideals. Such changes alter the Christian relationship, truly, but they also make it more positive. It may be argued that some aspects of inner development in Islam seem like a partial absorption of things Christian and that, as such, they may immunize the Muslim from complete and inclusive reckoning with Christ. But these fears are unworthy. There remains an even more wonderful relation in Christ to Muslim transformations of Islam than ever obtained to its perversities. Only the

[1] Lord Cromer, *Modern Egypt* (2 vols.), New York, 1908, vol. 2, p. 229.

new situation must be known imaginatively for what it is.

It may happen that the Christian endeavour to understand Islam to the full will result in Christian expositions of Islam that many actual Muslims would not recognize as familiar. The charge that this has occurred in Part 3 below is anticipated from some readers. But there is nothing surprising in this possibility: nor inappropriate. To see anything through Christian eyes is to see it in the light of Christ, and from the standpoint of 'the God of hope' revealed in Christ. What matters is that the exposition should be seen on reflection to have conveyed a true picture. No intelligent Christian takes as a criterion of theological validity the immediate reaction of some illiterate peasant to a statement of the faith.

Surely the living interaction of theologies means that committed and alert minds should delve into the other realm and bring the freshness of exterior criteria to what they find. The real test of the validly Islamic is not how the general run of Muslims would decide, on the spur of the moment. Little creative thinking within any system comes that way. Rather we must ask does the interpretation commend itself to a sensitive minority as the import or intention of what familiarity has obscured or disguised? The dissemination of the resulting sense of the thing must not be ignored or neglected. But the meaning of faiths does not first depend upon general and actual practice of them. Inter-religion in the creative sense is not a mass movement, though its servants will neglect the masses at their peril.

The other part of honesty is crisis. The word is deliberately used in preference to criticism since the latter has undesired implications and misses the ultimate point. It is not that the Christian has this or that to criticize: but that the whole of Islam must be for him under the decisions that arise from Christ, under judgment in the sense of crisis. The Christian understandings constitute for it a critical situation, a situation in which a wholly other set of criteria are given to it. This critical encounter is not the carping of Christians, nor controversy in the vulgar sense. It is simply the contrasts that are implicit in the nature of what Christ is and brings.

Too often we cheapen this crisis by misunderstanding its nature. We tend to concentrate on delinquency or compromise and so do not join the real issues. The Muslim has the legitimate complaint that what we criticize is not Islam. We often also overlook, as critics, the common incidence of evil and disloyalty already noted as part of inter-religion. Such criticism, moreover, is usually self-exonerating and provokes retaliation in kind. Our true task is rather to bring to bear the different criteria in Christ for men's self-judgment both as to doctrine and to life. This duty involves the utmost honesty, both with ourselves and with the Muslim. It requires that we refuse to identify what differs and that we act with the courage of the different as a conviction. There is little point in relating ourselves to an idealization which is not there, except in our imagination, and still less in grounding the relationship anywhere than in the fulness of Christ.

Here the humility of mind for which the first plea was made is the only sufficient safeguard. We have nothing that we did not receive. But this truth is two-sided. If the faith is not ours to hold with proprietary pride, it is not ours to serve with proprietary liberties. We are its creatures and disciples. As such, we must be loyal in and to the crisis Christ brings into all inter-religion. We cannot mistake that there is a difference between a revelation that contents itself with law, and a revelation that brings personality: that God in the Quran and God in Christ are God under seriously divergent criteria of Godness: that prophethood as finalized in Muhammad is in crucial senses discontinuous with prophethood as operative in Isaiah and Jeremiah: that the concept of Divine power as incompatible with an earth-dwelling enterprise is sharply contrasted with that of the Gospel where Christ crucified *is* the power of God. There can be no evading the realization that in Islam man's calling under God is differently conceived from his redeemed status in Christ: or that whereas the Divine mercy in Christ is pledged to man's renewal in grace, in Islam it is related in unpledged form to his pardon under law.

Some of these themes will be illustrated in Part 3. Christianity, in so far as it is loyal to its central meanings, brings a radical occasion of new self-assessment to all other systems of belief. But the nature of the Gospel is such that the impact of Christ is not totally to displace, but paradoxically to fulfil, what is there.

Take the example of the Messianic concept in the New Testament. For present purposes, it has affinity with the 'essentially religious idea of God reigning in the lives of men and in human society'[1] that Islam affirms. Within the 'hope' of the Messiah, as a heritage from Jewry and the Old Testament, Jesus came. Without that concept His advent and ministry would have lacked a framework and a link with earlier acts of Divine concern for man, of which His presence was the culmination. Within that concept, His purposes of redemption had close continuity with the minds and culture of his first hearers and disciples. In the context Messianism set for Him, He came fulfilling and achieving it. Thus the recognition of His identity as Messiah was the turning point in His education of His disciples.

[1] The phrase is borrowed from C. H. Dodd's description of the Christian meaning of 'the Kingdom of God'. See his *Parables of the Kingdom*, Nisbet, London, 1935, p. 35. The phrase is an example of how frequently Christian theology, in defining a Christian thing, may well produce what is also a feasible expression of an Islamic thing.

92

Conditions of Inter-Religion

Yet the concept and the whole context it provided were full of mortal peril for His mission and its goal. They were shot through with improper notions of victory, conquest, success, nationalism and revenge, wholly vitiating to the Christian nature of redemption. If He had answered Pilate's question 'Art thou a king then?' with an unqualified Yes! He would have admitted to Pilate's comprehension of Kingship. Had He denied with an unqualified No! He would have negated the royalty of the Cross. Hence the distinction about the sort of King He was – a subtlety, as it seemed to the Governor, with which Pilate had no patience.

But there was the dilemma. Not Yes! not No! rather Yes! and No! This issue, we are well aware, was faced in the inner education of the disciples. Somehow the fact of suffering as integral to Messiahship had to be worked into the scheme of things, for minds to which the two concepts were unthinkable together. The integrating of the two so that they were to be properly inseparable, was not fully achieved in terms of education. It came only after the event, in the Resurrection. Then the reality of such a Messiahship in the victory of a sufferer came unmistakably to light and it was seen to be gloriously in line with the earlier intimations of suffering kingship in Jeremiah and the Servant Songs in the Book of Isaiah.

Our Lord's relation to the formative concept-context of His whole mission was, then, one of realization by transformation. There was an irreconcilable hostility to the actual hopes about Messiah and a crisis of judgment upon them. Yet they provided the meanings and attitudes within which the judgment turned to salvation. For purposes of parable only (and without in any way equating the two elements in the parallel) we may say that the Christian Gospel has a similar concept-context in Islam. Its critical relation is

93

always constructive: its crisis always a crisis of hope. It quarrels with the Muslim concept only to propose a deeper significance to it. Such a conviction accords, not only with the nature of the two faiths in their separateness, but with all to which we have been led by thought on their involvement with each other.

These considerations have also led to the third quality of Christian relation with Islam. Humility and honest frankness must be active in theological translation. 'The sense of the word' we say, when we pause, maybe with a dictionary, over what precisely is meant by some term in question. If it is strange, we require to understand it by the help of what is already familiar. So with the sense of the Word made flesh. It is the heart of the whole Divine enterprise with which Christianity has to do, that God intends with men a relationship of knowledge, forgiveness and fellowship. The Gospel of the Word made flesh must be intelligibly told. Those who tell it must be prepared to reckon with the mental world of other men in which it is understood or – as often as not – misunderstood. From that world, the listener's world, comes the framework of ideas within which, at least initially, the new thing is judged. If witness is really translation, speaking to one realm the riches of another, it must attend like all other translations, both to what it says and how it goes.

As something existing for transmission – 'a faithful saying worthy of all acceptation' – the Gospel must enter other men's minds across the bridges its servants build into them. These minds must be fully known by its servants. For in the quality of their sense of how these minds think and decide lies, under God, the interpreted range of the Word itself.

The Gospel was always urgently interested in its hearers. Did not Jesus use parables to test and sift men's will to understand? Did not the early Church reach out eagerly into the

Gentile world to give the nations the fulness of Christ? Did not God Himself in the enterprise of the Incarnation come into the hearers' world, suiting His Word both to the Divine fulness and the human realm? It is 'the flesh' in St John's sense, that becomes the point of Divine-human translation. Continually then the bearers of the Word must bring their treasure and the ken of men together. Their task is to carry God's meaning into men's minds and hearts, that it may win their wills to obedience. All the resources of the Holy Spirit, working in us humility and fidelity, imagination and zeal, wait upon this task.

'THE SERVANT AS HIS LORD'

If these are properly described as the conditions of a Christian relationship to Islam, they are, like all other spiritual vocation, beset with temptations. It may illuminate and serve the situation if we recognize what these are. For much of the meaning of the Temptations in the wilderness has also to do with the Church. They concerned, in the experience of Jesus, alternative routes to His Kingdom, or alternative patterns of Messiahship. They epitomize the constant tests of truth. Corresponding paths of disloyalty open out in its own sphere before the Church. But unlike the Lord it all too often fails to recognize and renounce their falsity.

There is one popular form of inter-religion in our day which appears to have missed the point of the warning Jesus uttered in rejecting the temptation of bread in the wilderness. 'Stones into bread' was of course an excellent policy. The technology of our world today supplies an urgent and indispensable form of this miracle. Ways must be found to sustain the world's millions from the earth's resources. 'Stones into bread' is literally what technology achieves. Setting aside, for the moment, the aspect that has to do with

Jesus' own personal hunger and survival, and seeing the issue as a call to perpetual 'feeding the multitudes', this temptation is all too easily reproduced in the religious life of this scene and century.

Jesus was profoundly concerned about hunger; 'give ye them to eat' remains His command. But He was resolutely set against a campaign of merely material supply that evaded or ignored the deeper, spiritual needs of man, as a creature not 'of bread alone'. The prevailing technological revolution is sometimes urged as a reason for inter-religious co-operation. Let the faiths sink their differences in the new Leviathan and give their common attention to serving the goals of plenty, development and economic salvation. Let them unite to ensure, as much as in them lies, the better standards that will offset the blandishments of Communism and forestall the disruptive revolution it may otherwise inflict. This anti-Communist ground of inter-religious co-operation makes a strong plea to Islam and Christianity, since these have the common interest of their monotheism.

Co-operation to raise living standards and to disprove the Marxian thesis that redistribution of wealth must inevitably be violent, and for any other legitimate human purpose, is laudable and valid. Both Islam and Christianity are committed to their respective ideas of the just society. But the subtle point of the thesis, that turns into a temptation, is that religious co-operation in activism may fail men at the deepest level. If it involves them in a neglect of the dimension of worship or of the spiritual conditions of man's life under God, it lapses into what the Greeks called *polypragmosyne*, or 'multiplied doing' with the implication that meanwhile true responsibilities are being abandoned. It is relatively easy to bring religions together in such terms and at the same time relatively right. But unless the deepest meanings of faith for man's situation are undertaken the inter-religious duty is not done.

It may be that a negative form of this temptation comes in acquiescence at a sense of helplessness in face of the technological colossus, a posture of introverted pietism which concedes that materialist technology is all and does all. Such a tacit admission of religious irrelevance to life is an abdication both of duty and of faith. The temptation has become that of fear to survive on any but the world's terms. It should have the same courageous response that Jesus gave to the same suggested fear. That 'man does not live by bread alone' cannot be silenced as a warning, any more than it can be abandoned as an attitude. At all costs, our inter-religion must be more than doing things and more than leaving technology to do them.

The second temptation, in St Matthew's order, had to do with the compulsion to sheer credence. Descent from the pinnacle of the temple into the crowded court was calculated to assert Messiahship in a form involving no costliness in love or thought. The descending figure dropping unharmed into the midst would be authoritatively the Messiah. Perhaps. But he would never be authentically so. The kingdom must stand, not in an irrational credence of the overwhelming, but on the patient transforming ways of truth and life within the soul. Such an invocation of supernatural sanction by-passing the regeneration of the heart, had no place in the ways of God – a phrase which the tempter artfully omitted in quoting the Scripture for his purpose.

There are some forms of Christian preaching that have enough of the characteristics of this situation to warrant the parallel. It is no proper inter-religious relationship to preach impatiently an unexplained Gospel. 'The Word of the Gospel' refused to step commandingly into the world, but pursued the quiet patient processes which began in Bethlehem and went forward with obscure men, in a long and costly education the climax of which was the suffering of the Cross. 'I have given them Thy word', said Jesus. He did not do so in miraculous compulsion of their mental processes nor in an out-of-the-blue dictation of the unanswerable that left them still unregenerate and unpersuaded. His way was the involvement of loving personality with other lives, all the way to Gethsemane.

This is our only valid pattern. The Gospel in the trust of Christians in this multi-religious world cannot properly come with overruling compulsions of sheer authority. It must be ready to teach patiently and tenderly in the temple courts. It must cleanse them with its own infectious zeal. It must renounce the pinnacle and the invocation: 'Here it is; this is it; take it or leave it, but do not dispute it!' Merely asserting Messiahship in that impatient fashion was not being the Messiah. Likewise, asserting the Gospel is not preaching it.

The credentials of all faiths must be verifiable by inquiring minds. They must not be couched in some inaccessible form, like the claim of a Messianic pretender who descends from the pinnacle only because he cannot otherwise convince. Some expositions of Christian theology in world-relation really negate relation in the sheer authoritarianism with which they speak. A theology that is happy, even proud, to be allegedly discontinuous with all the conscious needs and actual thoughts of a religious world is not the Gospel of 'the Word made flesh'. Christianity succumbs to the second temptation if it refuses to commend itself in the utmost reverence for men's minds and wills and in a patient regard for their dignity and their religious heritage.

The meaning of Christ's rejection of the temptations is to be found in the course and pattern both of His teaching and

His passion. There we see the activity of a Gospel that is prepared, out of hiddenness and even disrepute, to seek recognition and its proper welcome, by dint of nothing save its own inherent significance, painstakingly related to all with whom it has to do. The Church likewise must repudiate all attitudes that draw their skirts around them and refuse to do more than dogmatize. For in Christ

> ... the divine is in disguise and no official mark of an external and independent authority can ultimately decide for us that the divine is there. There is a moral as well as a theological challenge in this, both in regard to Christ and in regard to the Holy Spirit. They must both be recognized by the intrinsic qualities that are theirs. They must speak with their own authority. The note of authority is indeed the one infallible mark of the divine – not the authority of the sergeant major, or of the totalitarian dictator, but of an inner compulsion which goes deeper and carries further, because it awakens that love which is the only fulfilling of the law. . . . The veritable signs of God's presence are intermingled with many other things. We walk with a stranger on the road to truth and all the evidence of identity given to us may be the heart that burns within.[1]

These truths are only the counterpart of that indispensable humility on which earlier pages insisted.

The third temptation is more subtle still. It was to have, or to seek, more than a servant's kingdom. 'Thou shalt worship the Lord thy God and Him only shalt thou serve.'

---

[1] H. Wheeler Robinson, *Redemption and Revelation*, op. cit., p. 296. This moving expression of the matter came to hand after the arguments of the preceding paragraphs had been set down. The two move in somewhat different realms. But all that Dr Robinson has to say about inner Christian recognition of truth applies even more strongly to our external relationships in truth. 'For us . . .' may read 'for them . . .' and the 'many other things' with which the signs of God's truth intermingle may be Islamic things. The point is that we cannot presume to be present, in a temper other than that in which God is.

The Messianic kingdom was not divisible with Satan, but tributary unto God. Its proper Lord was the Lord of the Servant, through whose fidelity it came to be. His fidelity is seen to be the form of the Divine victory. No Christian service, then, within that kingdom can properly be self-regarding. 'It is enough for the servant that he be as his Master.'

Precisely here our Christian involvement with other men in the crisis that the Lord Jesus brings may so easily work out to our own self-esteem. One of the deepest truths of Christianity is the endlessly regressive character of human self-centredness, making men proud of their humility, complacent that they are penitent, satisfied that they are orthodox. We are always tending to involve ourselves in the distinctive uniqueness of what we preach. We have need to remember Thomas of Canterbury's question when he first realized that even martyrdom might be self-regarding:

> Is there no way in my soul's sickness
> Does not lead to damnation in pride . . .?
> Can sinful pride be driven out
> Only by more sinful?
> Can I neither act nor suffer
> Without perdition?[1]

This tempter offers what we desire, offers what we serve, but centres it upon ourselves. If we submit we betray all. The only emancipation from the entail of the selfish self is to seek a wholeheartedly servant-status, in which the self is truly transcended and even its griefs and triumphs are not its own. For otherwise:

> They who serve the greater cause
> May make the cause serve them.[2]

[1] T. S. Eliot, *Murder in the Cathedral*, London, Faber, 1945, p. 40.
[2] *Ibid.*, p. 45.

100

Conditions of Inter-Religion

Here is the final crux of a Christian role in this inter-religious world. This is the ultimate condition of a Christian attitude to Islam.

Ours is a unique Gospel, which yet sternly forbids its disciples to 'thank God they are not as other men are'. We preach a universal crisis for all men in Christ. It may not be proclaimed in a manner which somehow exempts the heralds. We are tempted to be proud and patronizing about the good news of the lowliness of God. We are in danger of taking into our communal self-esteem the uniqueness that resides in One Who made Himself of no reputation. We properly inherit from the Divine initiative a corporate community of faith, yet we often act as though it were exempt from the law by which it came to be – the law of the corn of wheat that bears much fruit by giving itself away. We rejoice in the life of the new covenant and suppose it immune from the menace of self-content which was the undoing of the old. How easy it is to divert the interests of the Gospel to the interests of its people: to fail in the service of the Gospel because we succeed in its patronage.

The apostolic formula for Christian personal life was: 'Not I but Christ.' Then the authentic calling of a Christian community in the inter-religion of today is in the words: 'Not we but Christ.' Plural selves are more prone than private ones to miss the duty of losing themselves in what their selfhood serves. Or, in other New Testament language: 'Ourselves your servants for Jesus' sake.' All Christian thought about inter-religion leads back to that centre – Christ's sake and men's service. These, in turn, bring us again to sandals, other men's and ours, on the ways of the world.

PART 3

Present with the Peace of God

>>> ✧ >>>

'AND ALL HER PATHS ARE PEACE'

A SANDAL is a very prosaic thing, like the ass on which Jesus rode into Jerusalem to betoken the character of the Presence that brought crisis to the city. The simple things are biggest with significance.

What then of the sole of the soul with which the Christian walks in the world? Emerging from his reverent search for Islam and with the spiritual criteria of relatedness we have now studied, how does the Christian understand his responsible presence among his fellow-men in their religious diversity?

Footwear has the lowly function of perpetually conditioning the tread of the owner's feet. It interposes between him and all terrain. It mediates to him the vicissitudes of his pathway. Our Christian sandals, in a figure, brought us to the mosque door as careful students. How, in fact, do they take us thence into the world that flows beside the sanctuary? It happens that St Paul has a graphic phrase on this very topic. It comes in a context of military equipment which deserves to be seen as one whole. With 'the girdle of truth, the breastplate of righteousness, the shield of faith, the helmet of salvation and the sword of the Spirit' he lists 'the shoes of peace'. With all this weight and wealth of armour, the feet are of first importance. An unshod soldier is in as bad case as an ungirt one. His capacity to make good with righteousness, salvation and faith depends on his ability to keep on his feet, which will be thanks, surely, to his sandals.

The writer of the Epistle, however, is not content, as with the other items in the armoury, to speak simply of the piece and the purport: girdle – truth, breastplate – righteousness, shield – faith, helmet – salvation. He adds, in the one particular of the sole, an intriguing and suggestive word, tantalizingly rendered into English 'the preparation'. It clearly does not signify 'preparation' in the usual sense of the modern English word 'making a thing ready' or 'a concoction which is the result of such a process'. For the Gospel of peace is already given; its givenness is one of the biggest truths about it. As such it has no need to be prepared, like some schoolboy's exercise or a lecturer's discourse.

Happily it is just this 'givenness' which the Greek word implies. The Gospel is already there, as a man's shoes are when he crosses the threshold. Its prompt and constant availability is such that it is a perpetual equipment for what it requires, as sandals are for walking. The readiness of the Gospel of peace ensures that the Christian need never be at a loss in the relationship he must bear to others. The Gospel of peace is always there, ready, available, sufficient. In terms of it, like a well-shod pedestrian, he has his being, his being in relationship.

In that sense, the word 'relevance' perhaps yields the most satisfactory translation of St Paul's meaning: 'Have your feet always sandalled with the relevance of the Gospel of peace.' Or in larger paraphrase: 'Let the significance of the good news of the peace-making of God be your principle of adequacy in relation to every situation into which you go.' The force of the expression means there-at-hand-ness – a meaning fully confirmed in the metaphor of shoes. The terms of the Gospel are our abiding pattern of intercourse with men.

Present with the Peace of God

If we act upon this apostolic idea of the unremitting availability of the Gospel of peace, what will it mean *vis-à-vis*
Islam? What is the relevance of Christ as Christians understand Him to the inward Muslim meanings? How shall
these sandals of the peace of God walk in the world of the
mosque?

Reflection suggests that there are certain elements in the
Christian Gospel of peace that may be interpreted through
basic essentials in the meaning of Islam. St Paul's metaphor
has a fascinating bearing on the whole concept of *Islam*. It
is proposed to explore it here as a single, if inclusive, example
of what Christian communication may aspire to be and say
amid Islam. But first what is the nature of the peace that is
news in the Gospel?

Hasty judgment might suppose that being 'shod with the
sandals of peace' means entering into every situation with a
readiness for quiet compromise as if the Gospel meant an
avoidance of issues, and an uncritical will to acquiesce. On
the contrary, the good news begins by being disturbing. It
calls for surrender. The decision for repentance is a decision
against oneself. That He 'stirred up the people' was a charge
against Jesus Himself at the end of His ministry. His Gospel
will have no pacific relations with complacency and no
tolerance of self-satisfaction. It is a Gospel of peace only
because it is a profoundly disconcerting thing which comes
with radical judgment and transforming decision into every
situation. It is far from being an announcement of placidity
without revolution or of congratulation through self-
exoneration. That we need no criticism, no penitence, no
quarrel with what we are, no strife about what we have
been, can never be good news to any system or to any soul.
Only in its capacity to judge and disturb every complacence
does the radicalness of the Gospel bring newness of life. The

meaning of God's peace must be sought in deeper realms than those of easy co-existence between religions.

It happens that there is in jurisprudence a concept which comes effectively to our aid. One of its most familiar instances is the Anglo-Saxon notion of 'the king's peace'. Let us take the phrase, as being, somewhat diversely, a clue both to what Islam proposes and the Gospel announces. 'The king's peace' means the peace of sovereignty. It is the assertion of the reign and rule of law in the lives of men and societies. A glance at the historical origins of the idea makes a ready way to its essence. Maitland, the well-known English constitutional historian, describes how it emerged:

The idea of law is from the very first closely connected with the idea of peace. (No Muslim is likely to disagree.) He who breaks the peace, puts himself outside the law. He is outlaw. But beside the general peace which exists at all times and in all places . . . every man has his own special peace and if you break that you injure him. Thus if you slay A in B's house, not only must you pay A's price or wergild to his kinsfolk, but you have broken B's peace and you will owe B a sum of money, the amount of which will vary with B's rank. . . . Like other men the King has his peace. In course of time, we may say, the King's peace devours all other peaces.[1]

How this devouring may be held to resemble the Divine sovereignty in Islam, which devours all other sovereignties! Why the king's peace gradually superseded all other peaces involves a variety of reasons – the superior royal power in enforcing the royal peace and speedily righting or punishing infractions of it; the king's own desire for the revenues that accrued from offering a more effective justice; the steady decay of the feudal system with its hierarchy of men and

[1] F. W. Maitland, *Constitutional History of England*, Cambridge University Press, London, 1955 edition, p. 108.

'peaces'; and the general spread of kingly power and ambition.

Progressively, and, as seen in retrospect, inexorably, the king's peace displaced all other 'peaces' until the whole criminal jurisprudence was the king's. The Crown came to have a universal cognizance of cases. Its sovereignty in enforcement of the peace was well-armed with courts, judges, magistrates and penalties. For the king's peace, we must be clear, was militant. It took prompt and vigorous note of offences and offenders. Every disturbance of the peace was immediately its business. It was, at least in intention, as vigorously active against lawbreaking as Islam against idolatry – and for a not dissimilar reason. Within its domain it brooked no rival. It was a peace with sinews, a peace with sanctions, whose lawfulness had to be asserted against all comers. It was thus in turn a haven for the fearful, a terror for the lawless, a warning for the unruly and a refuge for the powerless. In the security it provided it expressed and ensured its own sovereignty. It brought a unity of legal will into the manifold of human affairs.

If peace is in this way the antiseptic quality of sovereignty, the capacity of law to become force as well as letter, right as well as writ, it provides a suggestive parallel for some fundamental Muslim ideas about the Divine sovereignty and the meaning of 'the peace of God'. Elsewhere St Paul refers to the latter as 'keeping a garrison' in men's hearts and minds (Phil. 4.7). His metaphor, paradoxically, is military. Again he exhorts: 'Let the peace of God rule in your hearts' (Col. 3.15). Such peace is the authority of the Divine will looking to its own order and asserting the power and love of that order against whatever presumes to disturb or defy it. Peace, in Divine terms, is far from being a precarious something that has itself to be carefully shielded and protected. It is rather the militancy of God's Kingdom against all that flouts its claim. The proclamation of the reality of this peace constitutes the good news in the New Testament.

There was majesty too in the King's peace. It rendered both obsolete and improper any pursuit of private rights or private vengeance. In like manner the truth of one God disqualifies all superstitious invocation of multifarious deities. The 'peace' delivered men from chaos, as monotheism delivered them from a chaotic worship. Its sovereignty satisfied all private wrongs by making them public, delivering men from the intolerable burden of their own avengings. Thus it protected the wrongdoer even in requiting him.

Its most condign punishment was outlawry, by which it exposed intractables to a status where they could legitimately expect the worst that private vengeance could exact. The outlaw was deliberately cast back into a state of pre-law, made all the more perilous by the withdrawal of the only protective authority which could restrain society's enmity. He lacked even the protection of ordered punishment and lay under a limitless curse. His lot was a total defencelessness, an unpitied rightlessness, among a people to whom juridically he had ceased to belong. The outlaw in these realms of ancient jurisprudence illustrates the truth that outside law there is only peacelessness. Here is the fulness of our present parable. For peacelessness is exactly what the Gospel goes out to overcome.

But there are important contrasts between this human parable and the Divine reality. The peace of God of which the Gospel tells never withdraws from man. Unbelief excludes itself. 'The kingdom of Heaven' in the glorious phrase of the *Te Deum laudamus* is 'opened to all believers'. The very preparedness of this peace is such that none need despair of it. All remain within its intention, be they rebellious or surrendered. Furthermore in the realm of the peace

108

of earthly kings are wide areas of life which do not concern the peace until it is breached, or which are not open to its writ because they are hidden in the recesses of men's souls. It is never so with the peace of God. In active energy it works to subdue all things to its proper rightness and their true wholeness.

Whereas, again, the king's peace has no trouble with the naturally law-abiding, it is otherwise with God's peace. Here we are all insubordinate and rebellious. We are all involved in evils that defy it. There is no end to its quarrel with our sins. If God's will to our being made right was as complacent as we often are about being wrong, how evil indeed would be our case. Or, putting the matter in another way, we may say that all law-abidingness with the peace of God is by inward revolution and the new heart, not by natural disposition or convention or mere lethargy of never doing (legal) wrong, as is so often the case with those who 'law-abide' the state.

These Christian insights will be clearer anon. Meanwhile we leave this somewhat extended analogy with apologies to the legists. With a little imaginative goodwill the point is clear. Islam itself as a term is often said by Muslims to mean 'peace' derivatively from the prior meaning of submission. A state of surrender means a resultant peace. The Muslim is the one in this peace of surrender. To pursue the point of our parable in the Muslim-Christian field, it is necessary first to explore the Muslim 'peace' of conformity to the Divine will. It embraces three basic elements – *Shirk*, or the disorder which is wrong; *Islam*, or the order that is right; and the *Muslimun*, or the community of this right order.

ISLAM AND MEN'S IDOLS

That the Prophet Muhammad was set for the overthrow of

idols is the most familiar of facts about his history. His supreme mission was the assertion of the sole sovereignty of God and His exclusive right to worship and service. A sense of the futility of idolatry seems to have been among the earliest and most formative factors in Muhammad's vocation. The darkest tragedy of his people, deeper than their tribal feuding and their disunity, which indeed it largely explained, was their multiplicity of deities. His contemporaries knew of a supreme God, but His very supremacy made Him peripheral in their thoughts, while the gods and goddesses of fertility, war and harvest, played an intimate role in their lives. The celestial non-entities received a more urgent and more wistful worship. To disqualify this intervening hierarchy of illusory beings was the Divine summons to the messenger and the messenger's summons to men. They had neither right, nor power, nor reality: to worship them was criminal folly.

Thus the great *Shadadah*[1]: 'There is no god except God.' The Prophet's early preaching was literally charged with this theme. Likewise the opposition – which only successful conquest terminated – sprang from the force of vested interest, tribal and economic, rallying, like the silver-smiths of Ephesus, to the defence of the deities whose shrines made Mecca famous. Only after resistance had been broken, eight years following Muhammad's emigration from it as a fugitive, did the city know that an idol-less sanctuary and a depaganized society would still have prosperous need of each other.

If the mission, the antagonists and the campaigns of the Prophet all had to do with this issue of God and the idols, it is natural that *Shirk* is one of the most passionate themes of the Quran. Derivatives, either nouns, verbs or participles, having to do with this term, occur some seventy-six times.

[1] The term means 'Confession of faith'.

But numerical frequency of mention matters only as the token of uncompromising hostility to the thing.

What then does *Shirk* signify? In origin it has affinity with the modern Arabic for a commercial company. The usual translation is 'association', with God understood. This is unfortunate: for God is far from being out of association with man. His will, His law, His revelation, His having an 'apostle', the Quran itself – all these, and more, in Islam, indicate that God has much indeed to do with man and man with God. Complete non-association would mean that religion itself, including Islam, was meaningless delusion. Nor is the real sense of *Shirk* the making of things equal with God (for this in truth is impossible since God is unmatchable: Surah cxii). It is rather the alienation of the only Divine. It means Divinity-status being falsely attributed to other than God. *Shirk* in thought and act is the attitude that pluralizes Godness and diverts in others directions the worship and reverence properly addressed to God alone. The anathema against *Shirk* did not set man and God out of all relation. It meant that man is properly related to God only when God alone is the one subject of his worship. Concisely put, it is not 'dissociation' which is right, meaning that God is withdrawn in aloofness, but *Tauhid*[1] the awed recognition that only God is God.

Islamic doctrine at its genesis in this denunciation of *Shirk* was about the God 'to end all gods', about God militantly disqualifying and annihilating all misdirected worship. Islam in concept is God being God in the right meaning of His jealousy and man being truly man in the single appropriate eternal relationship. *Shirk* as the antithesis of such

---

[1] *Tauhid*, another verbal noun, means the Oneness of God and its confession against all polytheism. It is the triumphant antithesis of *Shirk* and the deepest theme of Islamic theology.

rightness might occur, said the theologians, in a variety of forms. There was *Shirk* in the attribution to other than God, of knowledge such as only God possessed, or power, or capacity, or will, or worshipfulness.

Popular Islam in its superstitious forms finds emotional refuge in attitudes which, to the outsider, appear inconsistent with the disavowal of *Shirk*. If so, this is not the only area where emotional demands and theological consistency prove hard to reconcile. The Quran itself appears to validate and exemplify this tension. For on the one hand it defines the Muslim as he who fears naught save God (Surah ix.18) while, on the other, it encourages him to believe in the power, and to fear the influence, of jinns and other demonic agents. Certainly these beings are far short of Divine – the Quran itself is understood as being addressed to them as well as to men – thus emphatically including them within submission and creaturehood. But they tend to replace in the popular mind that idolatrous polydaemonism which Islam negated in the Prophet's Arabia. If no longer deified in imagination and belief, these creatures, apparently with Divine sanction, continue to play their role in popular Islam. If worship was not diversified, fears were. To that extent the sole fear of God is jeopardized and an aspect of *Shirk* creeps back in the very setting of its denial. Protective powers against jinns and other evil agencies are still widely attributed to amulets, jujus, charms and other items of Muslim superstition, when properly only God is the protector, sufficient and all-competent. The fears from which defence is sought have no existence save under Him.[1] The paradox is plainest

[1] The writer has often tried to ascertain from Muslims how these aspects of superstition might be justified as in no way involving *Shirk*. One of the most intriguing answers was one received from the Chief Imam of Ibadan, Nigeria: 'God doubtless is our sole protector,

when verses from the Quran itself are superstitiously used to do God's work of safeguarding the believer, when that Quran affirms that the feared entities have neither existence nor power save under Him.

Doubtless it is right to explain this phenomenon as a triumph of man's incurable will to pluralize, of his unwillingness to unify his fears or his trust. Yet it is by the prohibition of *Shirk* itself that we identify them as inconsistent. That principle is the true Islam, in its confidence that God needs no help to do His work and that His worshipfulness must never be diverted to another.

But of much more significance in the realm both of refined belief and of actual practice are the wide ramifications of this ruling invalidity of *Shirk*. Idolatry in the crude and literal sense is its simplest and least subtle form and may often be the least heinous. For idolatry, though rarely so, could in fact be merely a mathematical error – the instinct to gratitude and reverence wrongly diversified. It may well be, in other words, a right attitude too widely distributed. When unified, the sense of indebtedness and the yearning for a relation beyond the visible, that characterize the pagan, are still present in educated expression. The redemption of such idolatry may involve only an education in *Tauhid* or Unity, and a judicious iconoclasm. No doubt there is almost always something more reprehensible in practice about idol-worship as it obtains in paganism, since man's errors go far beyond mere number (cf. Rom. 1.18–32). But the point is

but He allows us to build houses and wear clothes to serve this protection.' Charms, likewise protect a man, but still leave him as God's protegé. But this, assuming we accept it, still leaves the question unanswered as to whether the fears themselves are valid. If only God is God, then only God is to be feared. As the Quran affirms, 'our only need of protection is from Him and is only found in Him' (cf. Surah ix.118).

worth making to throw into contrast the more radical reaches of man's deviations from a true worship, his chronic proneness to other gods that no external iconoclasm can correct.

To penetrate these reaches is to come upon the heart of the Islamic, and for that matter the Christian, quarrel with aspects of the modern world. What is wrong with an un-bridled nationalism that makes the ego of a single people or race the final criterion of existence and of action? Simply that man has deified his nationality, has made his racial collective into an idol, all the more menacing for being intangible and spiritual. If he is to repudiate this political and philosophical version of *Shirk* he will need more than an axe such as once shattered the gods of the Quraish. He will need to refuse to love his country with closed eyes or sealed lips. He will need to recognize the ultimacy of God beyond the partiality of race and the social collective. He will be obliged to see his nationhood under God and subject to the constant judgment of a Divine relation. Only so can he be truly a Muslim and a nationalist at the same time.

Contemporary Islam, as we have hinted above, has had large occasion for this issue by dint of its widespread, and proper, invocation of the spirit of nationalism as a means to the dislodging of Western imperialism. Many writers have sensed that there is a necessary spirit of imitation in this proceeding. Fewer have seen the tension it represents for traditional Islam. In any event, the anathema against *Shirk* – as the criterion of Islam – demands a vigilant subordination of any collective to the rule and priorities of God. In that sense, it remains profoundly exacting to be a Muslim. Being rightly submissive means not being wrongly submissive. There, indeed, is the rub, not only for tyrants but for all impatient men.

Or to go further, what is wrong with an unbridled commercialism? the attitude that demands only gain, sees only markets and proclaims that what is good for business is good? Simply that man has deified his profits and turned his gold into a god. Here too is a vicious instance of *Shirk*, and one hardly susceptible of merely physical eradication. The proper submission to God alone is seen to involve a resolute refusal of submission to practices that enslave man, or irreverently exploit and prostitute nature and so defy the image of God in human society. The recognized demands of God are the only safeguard of the valid dignities of man. Or as has been so often said, on Christian lips, only in worship, that is, in worshipfulness, can man be safe or saved.[1] There is a *Shirk* of the counting-house and the trade mart, as well as of the polytheist: a *Shirk* that outrages a true society as well as a true theology.

Or again, what is wrong with the Communist absolutism of the Party and the creed, with the totalitarianism that recognizes no judgment on itself, no terms of reference beyond its own sovereign self-assertion? Simply that in absolutizing its dogmas and its claims Communism has dethroned God. It is, of course, perfectly possible for a contra-Communism to be equally idolatrous, if it takes its ultimate criteria outside a state of valid submission to God (which will express itself in the acknowledgment of some validities in the Communist intention and in the recognition of the dimension of penitence). But whether Communism or its counter-ism, any absolutism that refuses God is *Shirk* and to allow it and pursue it is to be non-Muslim. *Shirk*, then, may be seen in the insistence that evil may and must be done that good may come, that Satan can somehow cast out Satan,

[1] This truth was integral to the thought, writings and discourses, for example, of Archbishop William Temple.

that the victories of justice must be loveless, that social righteousness can never be by regeneration but only by violent dispossession. For all these implications or assertions of the Communist have seriously dethroned God and taken unto themselves the gods of classlessness, war, violence and the ideological *élite*.

Islam is in the midst of a searching encounter with Communism, even if these its ultimate dimensions are rarely active in the great debate. Whatever may be said about the sociological or economic capacities of Muslim theory and institutions to provide adequate discipline for capitalism and adequate defences against Communism (which is a long story) the final and the prior issue will always be the spirit and sources of its contra-Communism. There can be no doubt that, authentically understood, antagonism to *Shirk* means such a contra-philosophy and counter-action. The Communist is without doubt a *mushrik*, an associator, in a far more desperate sense than the pagan. He has flouted the claim: 'Thou shalt have none other gods but Me', with a ruthless and defiant completeness. On this issue he is the violent and unrepentant antagonist of the Muslim, properly so called.

These are only examples, though crucial ones, of the reach of *Shirk* and the inclusive meaning of Islamic anathema upon it. They may be plainly reinforced by the Quranic narrative of the rebellion of Satan, or *Iblis*. In Surahs ii.34, vii.11–13, xv.30–32 and xxxviii.72–76, it is recorded how Satan demurred at God's action in setting a creature of dust in the earth. Man undertook 'the trust of God' (see Surah xxxiii.72) when all the world of nature had refused it. Thus man was called to have dominion, in God's name and in God's behalf, over the natural realm. Satan was prepared to express his disapproval (which other angels seem to have shared,

116

Surah ii.30) by refusal of obeisance. Was not God's act of trust in a creature so frail bound to miscarry? Was not the whole Divine idea of 'responsible mankind' ill-judged? So Satan registered a quarrel with God by rejecting acknowledgment of man's God-given status as *Khalifah*. For this insubordination to God, displayed in respect of the creature Adam, Satan was branded as rebellious and outlawed from Heaven. The implication seems clear. Non-recognition of man is non-submission to God. Satan's obduracy in rejecting prostration before man in recognition of his responsible dignity is Quranically understood as the crowning defiance of God.

The reach of this concept is immense. He who belittles the proper dignity of mankind, abnegates a proper devotion to God. This reciprocity in the situation is, of course, also thoroughly Biblical and Christian. But make no mistake. It is an assertion of the theological authority over all society, economics, politics and community. What our institutions and our theories make of man determines whether they are right with God. The sovereignty of God, so to speak, is staked in the dignity and vocation of man. To violate the second is to flout the first. The Divine Lordship which *Shirk* refuses, alienates and disallows, is pledged to the inalienable right of man as master-servant, properly the artifex över nature and the pontifex under God, bridging with his wisdom and his worship the rule of Heaven and the processes of earth. Man is king and priest, but neither in isolation. For he only truly rules when he validly praises, only governs as he kneels, only masters in that he prays.

Shirk, then, has this supreme corollary that non-recognition of man is non-submission to God. Tested by these criteria there is certainly no end to the range of its implication for life, society and the state. We need a sharpened understanding of who is the *mushrik*. We shall find him, find him out (if the reader prefers), in unfamiliar garb, but unmistakably guilty, in far more desperate places than an idol temple or beside the altars of an illiterate paganism. And conversely we shall have to assess who is the *muslim* by criteria that far transcend any superficial attachment to the mosque or the Shariah. If all this is disturbing to our familiar securities, it is no more so than was the original iconoclasm with which Islam first burst upon the world of the Quraish. If Islam is truly a universal faith, it must concern the idolatries that are universal – and universal not merely in their incidence but in their pervasive totality throughout human life and thought. Islam, by these reflections on its own meaning, is invited to a more radical loyalty to its own proud duty to have none other gods but He. 'Thou that abhorrest idols, dost thou commit sacrilege?' (Rom. 1.22).

THE SHAPE OF GOD'S KINGDOM?

These deep-rooted considerations have in a sense already anticipated our second theme – *Islam*. Yet we must attend to other and positive aspects of this great idea. To veto *Shirk* is the negative – though in the circumstances of Muhammad's mission the necessary – pattern of a great positive. 'There is no god except God' is only grammatically negative. In the formative Arabian context, and then for all time, it means 'There is only HE.' 'None but . . .' in an idolatrous setting is the form of an intolerant affirmative. So considered, *Islam*, as submissive recognition of the sole sovereignty of God, is the antithesis of *Shirk*. Our exploration of the far reaches of *Shirk* has terminated in new dimensions of *Islam*. How could it be otherwise?

For present purposes it suffices to consider a few ruling aspects of the *Islam* we have learned in grappling with *Shirk*.

Present with the Peace of God

The Quran proclaims the majestic power of God in creation. The crown of the universe is man the creature-master, whose status as God's regent (*Khalifah*) is seen by many in contemporary Islam as the charter of modern technology. There have, it is true, been long stretches of Muslim theology which questioned man's rational competence and even disavowed such basic scientific concepts as causality, because they seemed to contravene God's sole right to create. Islam today is sure that in science man pursues and fulfils a destiny deriving from God. But the authority man wields, his dominion over things, are an empire that must recognize the duty of subjection. Man is truly over things because he is under God: the latter status gives meaning to the former.

The double direction of man's dignity which makes Islam, both requires and receives revelation. If man had no empire there would be no material for his obedience to God. If in authority over this material he had no vocation to submission there would, likewise, be no *Islam*. The recognition of God is made *by* man, *over* nature, *in* the setting of nature and mankind. It is the mutuality of man and his context, and both under God, that makes the arena for Islam.

So the Divinely given law comes to guide man the servant precisely because so great a dignity and duty are committed to him. The Quran is the *Furqan*, or criterion, by which man may know what to make with it. Amplified by the Sunnah or Tradition and other sources of Fiqh, or jurisprudence, the demands of the revealed law bear upon man's behaviour and the appropriate pattern of his response is the submission that the law categorizes.

Those demands are in part ceremonial. Three Pillars of religion namely, *Salat*, *Ramadan* and *Hajj* (worship, fasting and pilgrimage), are ritual demands, the other two being, one credal, and the other economic or social (*Shahadah* and

119

Zakat). But within this ceremonial pattern are clear moral and religious attitudes which the ceremonial actualizes and sacramentally realizes. These have to do with man's God-wardness in self-discipline, history and community. They aver in symbol and they discipline in practice man's recognition of God. The postures of prayer are a sacramental repudiation of *Shirk*: the privations of the daily fast during Ramadan assert the primacy of the spirit: participation in the Pilgrimage links Muslims in space and time to the one place and point of the revelation they follow. What is confessed in witness, performed in prayer, admitted in alms, disciplined in fast and sealed in pilgrimage, is the believer's acceptance of the status of a submitted one. These Pillars of Religion are the religious 'ought' which focuses and hallows, and so enables, the ethical 'ought'. On these Pillars the structure of submission thus is built.

But pillars are not the whole of any building, unless it be a ruin. The structure riding on these columns houses a whole social, political and cultural expression, thought of through all its ramifications and vicissitudes as the household of the Divine rule. It has doubtless gathered to itself many items of emotional and communal belonging which might be thought dispensable, or even deleterious to its avowed meaning. There is never any respite from the task of the reformer or renewer. There must always be controversy about the details of this overall intention of Islam unto *Islam*. The one is shaped by and lives in the other.

Here then is the Islamic concept of the rule of God, bearing upon man's whole existence as creature-master-servant, in the context of time and nature. It is a scheme of accountability. The eschatological theme of judgment was a vibrant element in its early enunciation and remains a re-iterated burden of the Quran. God is the term of reference of our existence. All other contexts, personal, racial, communal and historical, find meaning in this Divine direction of our existence. Something that begins to look like 'a king's peace' emerges from our scrutiny of Islam. But we must resist the immediate pursuit of the suggestion (on which these paragraphs have been steadily converging) until we first complete our analysis by expounding the *Muslimun*.

In several senses the job is already done. But the corporate aspect must have its place. In derivation *muslim* is the active participle – the doer, while *Islam* is the verbal noun – the thing done. *Muslimun* (pl.) are the personal, corporate exemplars of Islam. They are a highly self-conscious community in the Quran. Historical circumstance at the Hijrah caused them to fall into the main groups, the *Muhajirun* and the *Ansar*, the emigrants and the hosts, the refugees and the helpers, the Meccans and the Medinans. But this differentiation was inward only: externally the *Muslimun* were in sharp contrast with all non-Muslims. The Quran is full of this antithesis between gainers and losers, the graced and the wrath-incurrers, the prospered and the misdirected.

This sense of the particularizing mercy shaping an initiate community is strong in Islam. Indeed it may be said to be the corollary of the very self-consciousness of Muslims as such. What they are excludes what they are not. Wide areas of the Quran and of Muslim thought seem to imply that the are-not-Muslim status of the non-submitters derives from the Divine decree operating through their own obduracy. Elsewhere it is recognized that 'it was their own selves they wronged' (cf. Surahs ix.70, vii.178 and vii.161 and many other passages) – implying that man's choice of disobedience is something other than the arbitrary fiat of God. But the election of the Muslim community does not allow any arrogant assurance. The status of being Muslim is itself within the disposal of God. Hence the reiterated and often anguished petition of Muslim prayer: 'O God, let me die a Muslim.' Hence also the reluctance of many theologians to admit the confession: 'I am a Muslim' but only, in its place: 'I am a Muslim if God has so willed,' the proviso being seriously important.

Yet, if unassured in any presumptuous sense and always *sub judice* until eternity, the status of the Muslim is none the less real. Creaturehood, obligation, weakness, frailty, allegiance – all these belong to it. This creature under law is perfectible but admittedly not perfect. The Quran recognizes the weakness of man and his forgetfulness. It is in these terms that it tends to explain his failure to achieve a steady *Islam*. Though in one place (Surah xii.53) the Quran makes Joseph (Yusuf) confess that man has a bias or proneness to evil, the Islamic view in general seems content to diagnose the wrongfulness of persons and society as arising from man's inherent feebleness rather than his active rebellion.

What arises, then, from forgetfulness can be countered by reminder. It is a matter of sins, rather than of sin: of lapses rather than of self-assertion. The whole aim of communal allegiance in Islam is to discipline, succour and educate that frailty. Thus salvation is largely communal. The exhortation of the sermon and of the Tradition and the numerous other features of belonging discussed in Part 1 are all calculated, through habituation, sound breeding, and communal attachments, to obviate lapses and ensure or serve ethical conformity. The Pillars of Religion are pillars too in the devotional sense, in that by reiteration and emotional renewal they help to actualize what they enjoin. Their discipline makes tangible the claims of God. Their fulfilment gives embodiment to the law.

Thus the achievement of *Islam* presupposes and requires

122

the community. It is in the total context of the ever-mediated past and the personal present that the community of the *Muslimun* has being. They constitute, as a totality, the household of the Divine law, the repository of the revealed pattern, the integration and perpetuation of the meanings that make them. The people of the faith are the crux of its continuity. In submitting, they gave, and give, concreteness to their master the law. Where the sources of law needed to be complemented and its silences interpreted, the community was the court of appeal, or at least of custody. The authority of their consensus it is true was only made articulate by the experts, the exegetes and pundits who qualified to be initiators of a communal mind. Such was the will to fixity or the fear of innovation that the community through many generations was thought of as being completely under the spiritual mortmain of earlier generations. Though in these ways far from any easy notion of democracy, or referendum, the concept of *Ijma* or consensus came finally to rest (as in the end all authority must) upon the will or soul of the believing people. Islam, both for practice and definition, stands, in the last analysis, upon the *Muslimun*. Islam is not only what God requires: it is what men do.

Another aspect of the place of the community of obedience takes us to the realm of the political. God's rule, as we have seen, demands man's submission. But man's being capable of fully making it, requires certain external conditions. The pre-occupation of Muslim thought with these conditions is simply the other side of its confidence that there are no inward conditions of an exacting kind – regeneration or radical transformation. Man is perfectible but the conditions of his perfectibility are environmental, circumstantial and thus also political. The context of devotional practice, as we have seen, is indispensable. But the achievement of Islam is far from being only a religious matter. Habituation and the opportunity to be validly what a Muslim should be require the Islamic political order. The faith must fashion and control the state. The state must be the instrumentality of the faith. The creed presupposes rule: government enables obedience. Man in Islam can only truly be himself when the appropriate Islamic conditions in the state are realized around him.

The actual form of this indispensability of the state has varied in Muslim history. For centuries the orthodox belief was that the Caliph was a *sine qua non* of a valid Islam and the essential guarantor of the whole community. There is a widespread tendency these days to forbear defining the Islamic state too rigidly. But behind the new nationalisms is the conviction that statehood is necessary to religion. And conversely so much diagnosis of the Muslim failure to be adequately Islamic takes the student, not to the revolt of man, but to the malaise of the state. For some critics there has been no adequate Islamicity since the days of the second Caliph, Umar – not because man has a radical wrongness, but because the Umayyads started a political rot long perpetuated and all too obviously bedevilled further by the alien imperialisms of modern times.

There is at least a consistency in this diagnosis. For if the non-attainment of an authentic Islam is politically explicable, then the kingdom of the Divine law and the external order could, presumably, be coterminous – an assurance no Christian diagnosis of man could accept. This belief that the political expression and the rule of God can coincide has been the ruling characteristic of Muslim belief about society and the Muslim hope about history. On the negative side, no separation between the realm of religion and the realm of the state is proper or tolerable (though the shape of the connexion is variable and debatable). Islam exists to be not only a way of devotion, but a form of government. It expects the rule of God, not only over, but as, the kingdom of men. The potential identity between them was the original keynote and the perpetual ambition of Muslim history.

Here, then, within the cramping limits of a few paragraphs, is the meaning of the faith of the mosque – of *Shirk*, its clue to evil, of submission, its condition of rightness, and of the *Muslimun* as the community of the good life and the political commonwealth of the rule of God realizable in this world. Here is the Shariah-salvation, the rightly guided corporateness, the embodiment of the intention of revelation. Here is the *ecclesia* or living organism coming and continuing to be in conformity to the Divine will, which, simply in being revealed, creates in devotion, government and popular practice the simple conditions of its own realization in law, life and behaviour.

There can be no doubt about the tremendous nature of what we have now outlined. Here is a magnificent idea. 'The term "Kingdom" (of Heaven)', wrote Professor C. H. Dodd, 'indicates that . . . in which God is revealed as King or sovereign Lord of His people or of the universe which He created.'[1] He is discussing the groundwork of the New Testament and the inner core of the Christian evangel. But the words are definitive, as they stand, of the Islam we have now studied. If it be objected that there are whole areas of Muslim life where secularity has obscured, if not defied, this definition, it must be understood that we are defining *Islam*. These evidences of defiance of its meaning are part of the context of struggle and relativity in which such a faith could not fail to be involved in a world like ours. If we refuse to define Islam ideologically and prefer to insist that there is

[1] C. H. Dodd, *Parables of the Kingdom*, Nisbet, London, 1935, p. 35.

nothing but struggle and delinquency, do we not really dissolve the whole situation, including the failures? We cannot in the end have the realism about what Islam is not (if such be our chosen emphasis) unless we have the ideology that allows us to be realistic. To deplore that Islam does not correspond to this rule of God but rather lives only in compromise is to make indirect acknowledgment of the Islam we have defined. We only know what it is not, by what it ought to be. As to which of the twain is Islam, the cynic will no doubt be certain, and perhaps as certainly wrong.

If it be objected that there are serious intellectual accounts of Islam – as distinct from spiritual failures – that repudiate some features of this analysis and that disqualify by their timidity or their rigidity some areas here characterized as Islamic, this may be honestly conceded. But again, we land ourselves in the ultimate question as to what is Islam. On that score, it would be idle to ask for perpetual unanimity among Muslims. The outsider's task is to do all in his power to ensure that his evaluations are fair, judicious and compassionate, that he hearkens to the intention which Islamic thought has made central to its Pillars, as well as to the unfulfilled, and that he brings qualities of heart commensurate with the mysteries of the world and the finitude of men.

Let the carpers grow more truly realist and they will walk more wisely with the sandals of peace. High time it is that we returned to those symbols of a Christian presence amid Islam. What is the meaning of the Gospel of peace to this Muslim submission, this vocation of responsible man to the Divine relation, this system of inclusive accountability to a single worship? Perhaps the reader has sensed already the rich potential occasion of Christian relation in this account of Muslim meanings. Perhaps, with apologies to Emily Dickinson, the Christian may say:

Present with the Peace of God

> I felt a kinship in my mind
> As if the truth had knit:
> I aimed to match it, seam by seam,
> To see how 'peace' would fit.
>
> The thought behind I strove to join
> Unto the thought before,
> And sequence opened out for me
> Like keys that turn a door.[1]

THE SHAPE OF A CROSS

As we saw, the peace of God initiates peace-making and goes out in sovereignty against all defiance of its authority. It takes note of all that is contrary and acts to subdue it into a proper unity of order and obedience. The meaning of the peace of God is that He must reign, that He subdues all things unto Himself having to do with men His subjects, but does so consistently with their status as men and His nature and character as God. The good news of peace is that God is not remote, aloof, negligent, but alive, cognizant, active and able. His justice is militant and His compassion enterprising. It is good news about God's unity, not in any barren, propositional sense merely, but in the sense that God wills to be

[1] Emily Dickinson, most wistful of American verse writers, lived 1830–1886 in Amherst, Massachusetts, and became a master of haunting, often monosyllabic, always lyrical, poetry. The poem here adapted is quoted from *Poems by Emily Dickinson* edited by M. D. Bianchi and Alfred L. Hampson, Little, Brown and Co., Boston, 1937, p. 49. It runs:

> 'I felt a cleavage in my mind
> As if my brain had split;
> I tried to match it, seam by seam,
> But could not make them fit.
>
> The thought behind I strove to join
> Unto the thought before,
> But sequence ravelled out of reach
> Like balls upon the floor.'

all in all by a great reconciling initiative, taking redeeming action about the human rebellion which, unredeemed, would perpetually flout the unity of His rule and the authority of His love.

That 'God is One' in this good news means not simply that there is metaphysically no other deity, which is true enough; but that He is set to bring under the one Lordship all alienating worships and all the insubordination of sin. God's unity in the Christian Gospel is not simply a unity that *is* but a unity that *acts*: not merely a majesty that dogma asserts, but a royalty that gloriously asserts itself in those blessed initiatives of grace which His own nature and our human *lèse-majesté* as sinners alike require.

This relevance of the Gospel of peace to the Islamic belief about the rule of God poses for the latter three questions, each of them fellows to each other. They belong in an integral way to what Islam is getting at. Each takes us into the heart of the Christian good news about God. They are: Is the human situation adequately mirrored in Islam? Is the Divine sovereignty sufficiently sovereign? Has our personal predicament its full answer? They must be examined with largeness of heart. They belong to the kindred Muslim-Christian awareness of the universe and arise out of the common involvement in which we are, as men, under God in this world.

Is the human situation adequately mirrored? Man in Islam has, as we have seen, immense if sometimes dogmatically compromised, dignity. *Islam* as submission, is something which men must bring – and so may equally withhold. The most inclusive and abiding of decisions is man's to make or not to make. Whatever else an automatic, inevitable conformity to eternal will might be, it would not be *Islam*. Man has this dignity of being accountable to God with an inclusive obligation which revelation guides, warns and informs. The accountability relates to all the concentric circles of his existence – personal, domestic, communal, economic and general. It is hallowed and betokened in a setting of devotional allegiance. It is sealed and enjoined by the corporate, historical continuity which is Islam. 'Guide us in the straight path, . . . not the path of those who incur Thy wrath nor of those who wander astray' (Surah i.7). All this the Muslim feels is gloriously valid. But has it mistaken the dimensions of our predicament?

This confidence in a solution to our waywardness in terms of guidance – has it measured the stubbornness of our sin? 'The good that I would' might be taken as a description of *Islam*. We are deliberately leaving aside here the Christian-Muslim issues about the content and locus of the law of God – in the one, personal in Christ, in the other, codal in the Holy Quran and Shariah. There are obviously serious distinctions in the whole ethical range and temper of the two faiths, and of law as law. But agreeing to concentrate here on 'the good that I would' however conceived and exemplified, what of the fact that I do it not? Clearly this refusal of obedience is vital to Islamic thought, because it involves a failure to surrender. To fail to face it is to abandon *Islam*. The nature of evil cannot be for the Muslim an academic issue. It is crucial to all that he is because by it the whole concept of Islam must stand or fall.

Islam, in general, is aware that there are conditions for the doing of 'the good that I would', the law that I recognize. They are, as we have seen, political, educational, communal and environmental. The Islamic stress on exhortation and habituation we have noted. It is thus fully admitted that men's capacity for non-Islam, their chronic proneness to some form of *Shirk*, are pervasive and mischievous. Islam

I

has not blindly believed in the docility of man – witness its insistence on the pre-requisite of the state. Some writers like Al-Ghazali have penetrated far into the psychology of temptation and the inward mysteries of iniquity. But for all that, Muslims have not admitted the radical measure of this problem. They have refused what they regard as the pessimism of Christian diagnosis and held stubbornly to the natural feasibility of Islam. They have remained broadly optimistic, in the good company of Greeks and many moderns, that the human predicament is savable in terms of knowledge only. Ignorance is our worst enemy – an enemy which revelation vanquishes, and in so doing meets our case. Thereafter, with the law in our hands, it is a matter of fidelity and all the apparatus of religious tutelage, plus the proper external government ensuring the pre-requisite conditions.

Are these criteria of the attainment of the good life sufficient to the actualities of human nature? Is not the situation rather like that described by George Herbert:

> Parents first season us: then schoolmasters
> Deliver us to laws: they send us bound
> To rules of reason, holy messengers. . . .
> Without, our shame: within, our consciences
> Angels and grace, eternal hopes and fears.
> Yet all these fences and their whole array
> One cunning bosom-sin blows quite away.[1]

When 'the bosom-sin' or man as he is in his rebellious self-assertion has defied our rules and laws and traditions, is the only answer redoubled exhortation, intensified sermonizing, renewed sanctions of warning and appeals of Paradise? Or these, and a sharpened effort to expel imperialism and erect the Islamic state? Are we to concentrate our search for

[1] Quoted from 'Sinne' in George Herbert, *The Temple*, London, Seeley and Co., edition of 1906, p. 60.

130

goodness on the remedies that only involve others, exempting and exonerating ourselves, or at any rate, the innermost part of us? Must the diagnosis of the wrongness of society always be external? Have we taken the measure of what we are, if we suppose that nothing need be done about our nature? Is it not manifest in all honesty that beyond the question: What is the good? which revelation and the law have answered, lies the question: Whether the good? which law alone, as St Paul saw so long ago, is powerless to realize.

We only take these questions into the Divine sovereignty, which assuredly they concern, when we ask God reverently as to their answer. Is the Divine sovereignty as Muslims conceive it sufficiently sovereign? The question from one point of view is blasphemous. There is none save He. His sovereignty is, therefore, total and being unrivalled cannot be inadequate. But in the concrete the question persists. Does this real situation of human non-Islam, of self-deifying *Shirk*, of God-defying sin, have no more than a revelatory reaction from God's side? That is to say, is the relation of His sovereignty to this state of affairs that defies Him merely that of the legislation by which the defiance is convicted as such? Is God related to our evil only in terms of a good law which identifies it for the wrong it is? For if so, then He is manifestly incompletely sovereign.

This is the whole significance of the metaphor of 'the king's peace' as a clue to the Gospel. No lawgiving can be indifferent to infraction. A law that is negligent about the insubordinate rapidly becomes no law at all. Law must rule as well as enjoin. God's peace must be action, or it ceases to be concept. Even the king's peace has to act and does so, relatively and juridically, in courts and verdicts. How much more must the peace of 'the merciful Lord of mercy'? Sovereign peace is interventionist: for its own sake and in pursuance of its own authority. Likewise must the sovereignty of God be interventionist, beyond law only and beyond revelation and beyond, in the merely punitive sense, all judgment.

If the sovereignty of God really has to do with the realm of man and if humanity is the material of its very majesty (as subjects are of kings), then it has to do redemptively with that realm and material. This is the message of the Gospel to the splendid conviction of Islam. God must reign and humanity is the dominion of His government. But this material is not automatically ruled and rulable, like planets, atoms, stones and trees. Nor is it merely to be regulated, checked and restrained like the citizens of civil states whose business is with public order, decency and justice. These cannot penetrate the inner recesses of the human soul that are most significant for God. Rather the writ of God must run beyond the limits of the prudential and utilitarian, into the realms where men's ultimate decisions are made, into the warped wills where acts of *Shirk* are born, into all within that, by its preference of self to God, means a willed deviation from His exclusive worship.

Men who have organized their universe around the centre of themselves and not of God, men in their ultimate non-Islam, can only be won again to submission by a Divine strategy that recognizes their freedom, the freedom in which alone a human submission can be brought, the freedom in which man wills to be a true, not a usurping, servant-master unto God in His world. So to win him must surely be the objective of a Divine sovereignty that cares about his true Islam. Only when man is truly man, man in the free and blessed pattern of the Divine intention, is God known as God in realized *Tauhid*. The good news is that, because He is fully God, He takes the initiative by which man can be restored to his true manhood.

That initiative means more than revealing the true. Law proclaims the rightful and identifies the wrongful. No more. Judgment alone annihilates the situation. Only redemption suffices – an enterprise for man's remaking that, within the condition of freedom, saves man from himself and restores him through pardon and newness of life to his status in fellowship with God. Such an enterprise has been undertaken. God in Christ is the God to end all gods. In the Incarnate Saviour, God reconciles the world unto Himself in the only adequately Divine counter-action to the challenge of 'the gods' – the gods of self and sin, the idolatrous substitutes in which all evil consists. It is hardly strange that the first Christians were widely accused of atheism. For to be reconciled by God in Christ was to have done with the multifarious and fraudulent deities of the secular and self-centred world![1] Yet passing strange that the Gospel of the Divine initiative for a unity of redemption should have been mistaken for a piece of polytheism. The truth was that the majesty in Heaven had also come, lowly, to earth, in order to remain, meaningfully, in Heaven.

The Gospel of the New Testament faith is a Gospel of peace-making by Divine intervention. The Christian conviction is that herein is God God. God, Who made man in His own image only to be denied by man the loving fellowship that was the goal of creation in freedom, yet more wonderfully restores him. In so doing, He made 'Thou shalt have none other gods but Me' a Gospel as well as a command and

[1] Cf. Charles N. Cochrane, *Christianity and Classical Culture*, New York, Oxford University Press, 1944, p. 225: 'The historical Christ was the "only Son" of the Father and so quite literally the God to end gods. It thus underlay what was commonly regarded as Christian atheism. For to accept this thesis was to reject as fraudulent the multifarious deities of secularism and in particular the claim to divinity put forward on behalf of . . . Caesar.'

133

a promise big enough to dethrone the most tenacious of the 'other gods' whose seats are wills and selves and societies, not rocks and stones and winds. Theologically stated the Christian faith is about a Divine unity that acts against its deepest rivals. In personal terms, it is an offer of forgiveness and the remaking of the heart in which 'thou shalt have no other . . .' becomes 'I will none other . . .'. 'Whom have I in Heaven but Thee?' 'Lord, to whom shall we go, Thou hast the words of eternal life.'

Is it surprising that in the terms which most validly proclaim Divine sovereignty man's personal predicament finds its total answer? The way of a legal moralism leaves the sensitive soul oppressed with its past failures. The opened Kingdom of pardon and peace sets men free from the accusing thraldom of what they have failed to be. For God was willing to accept them as they were. His relationships being those of redeeming grace, they did not have to undertake the hopeless task of qualifying in order to qualify. If one is standing on a character to be attained, one is already in bankruptcy. The prodigal son could never have returned, if his only hope was never having been prodigal.

Such a redeeming forgiveness does not establish a calculus by which we can never merit that the promise be ours, as does the ground of law. It freely comes to us, bidding us believe we have it and encouraging, not forbidding, our assurance. It has already itself carried our sins in the event of the Cross. Its mercy is open to all who will receive it. There is no unpredictability about its being ours. The conditions of its active benediction in our souls lie only in our will to penitence.

The peace of this Gospel reaches down into an adequate sense of how wrong I am. As long as I stand before God on the ground of law, I must know how the sin even in my law-abidingness condemns me. My self-centred righteousness rebukes me, unless I be in the still worse case of not being aware of it. 'O wretched man that I am! who shall deliver me?' This endlessly regressive character of human sinfulness, noted in Part 2, means that my responsibility goes back beyond what I do, to what I am; beyond what I observe (as law), to what I think. In these ultimate reaches of my lawlessness, and so of my violation of God's sovereignty, no law as such can ever save me. For they arise from the unsatisfied and unsaving law. My case is such that God must transmute my sinfulness into pardon and my selfishness into love. The work of His redemption is to break the bondage of my self-centredness and so bring me into the beatitude of His true Lordship, and into love of Him as the fulfilment of the self He made for love.

That in Christ this Divine work is accomplished is the good news of peace – the peace of personal wholeness for man and of the acknowledged worship of God. The place of its accomplishment is the Cross. For so great, so Divine, a work cannot but be infinitely costly. Forgiven-ness always flows from forgiving-ness. The Cross is simply, and sublimely, the inclusive point and passion of such a forgiving-ness, Divinely wrought in the context of the characteristic deeds of the sins to which it relates. 'Father, forgive them' is the plea of Jesus: His death is the event in which its answer is there given in the heart of God revealed in those very words. If it is the Muslim sense of the adequacy of law alone, and of a mercy that has no Cross at its heart, which makes the Christian faith in Christ crucified so strange an enigma, then, by the same token, that faith must be the heart of the relevance of the Gospel of peace to men in Islam.

These are the terms of a Christian presence amid Islam, purposely concentrated into their essentials and conceived within the conditions of religious relationship already discussed. Here, it would seem, is the shape of the meaning of God in Christ and Christ on the Cross to the business of the mosque. These are the sublimities that await our simple sandals and our common walk. For here in Christ is the last answer to the innermost idols. Here is the law of love to end (fulfil) law. Here is the action of God to end (dethrone) gods. To know this peace is to know how great is God, and how sovereign. It is to have discovered a true submission wherein God is indeed God and I am truly man. In such knowledge there is a trust of truth that puts 'shoes on the feet' (Luke 15.22) and betakes me joyously to my fellow men.

BUT . . . ?

There besets this whole conclusion, however, one urgent question. If an active righting of the world is so crucial to the sovereignty of God, why does the redemption in Christ appear often unsuccessful? If we insist that since law is flouted, there must be a re-making of the heart, why do we not face the fact that it seems to make so little difference? We assert that man because he violates the very good he approves has deeper needs than revelation satisfies. But is the enterprise of reconciliation any more effective in ensuring the good life and the true society? Has a Gospel of pardon more success than a law of submission? The true enthronement of God – 'the God to end gods' and the restoration of the one right worship – are these any nearer on Christian terms?

Is exhortation to obedience in Islam in any worse case than exhortation to conversion in Christianity? Is not the natural man as dominant and as determinative of things and of himself, whether we hope him perfectible or proclaim him fallen and invited to newness of life? The mystery of the

136

unredeemedness,[1] not least of the Christian world, seems sadly to jeopardize the New Testament announcement of the peace of God. Muslims genuinely suspect that this is the Achilles' heel of the Christian scheme.

Heel is perhaps a good allusion, since we are talking about feet and their armour. But do not these queries menace the underlying assumptions of Islam as well as Christianity? If we must write off God's ways with men as failure, or suppose that His righteousness is defeated, we abandon both our faiths. We can only face this problem of human non-Islam, of history's seeming rejection of the things of peace (be they law or grace), if we believe in Divine sovereignty. Only on such an assumption do the questions make sense. If God is not supposed to reign, there can be no 'mystery of iniquity'. If the problem is real, it is only because the conviction about Divine Lordship is real. The very burden of the problem is, in fact, the other side of our conviction that God is, and that He is almighty. If the Christian concept is groundless, what is at the heart of Islam about God can hardly breathe more easily. Rather it is likely to expire.

Islam has always believed that the Cross of Jesus ought not to happen: which is perhaps one way of insisting that if it did, it ought not to be a fruitless failure, an utter extinction barren of consequence. Love ought not to be worsted, says the Muslim. Hence Islam rescues Jesus prior to the Cross. By the same token, all the more, if the Cross happens, love ought not to be worsted beyond it. Further, to be sure, as

[1] The word is owed to a Jewish expression of the same problem, born out of the tragic Jewish suffering at the hands of the European world. Cf. Martin Buber, quoted in *Middle East, World Center*, New York, Harper, 1953, by Samuel Hugo Bergman in 'The Phenomenon of Israel': 'Standing bound and shackled in the pillory of humanity, we demonstrate with the bloody body of our people the unredeemedness of the world.'

Muslims are, that no means of forgiveness are necessary for God does not accord with the notion that the Divine will, engaged in a redemptive enterprise, might find itself frustrated. Muslim views of God have serious stakes in the Christian ones.

But these considerations, valid as they are, do not give the answer. They are observations about our interrogatives. The Christian response to these takes us back to the meaning of human freedom. Man's redemption involves the freely willed acceptance of the terms of his remaking. Clearly they cannot be compulsive. For then they would destroy the fellowship between God and man and the responsibility which is man's dignity. 'Behold I stand at the door and knock.' The Saviour Who has taken the radical measure of our wrongness brings His kingdom only to the penitent, while the Cross at its heart enables the penitence through which the Kingdom comes.

The Gospel of grace, then, has a different relation to man in evil than has law. Even where man's defiance continues, there is a large difference in what we defy. Law informs our ignorance and when the problem is no longer ignorance, but obduracy, this it will rebuke and condemn. Then the gulf widens and the righteousness of the law goes, by the way of the law, ever farther from our reach. If we acquiesce in this situation we are complacent sinners: if we deplore it we are despairing ones. The Gospel of grace is beyond this dilemma of the law. It assures us in the Cross that it reaches beyond our despair, while leaving us no ground for refuge in complacence. In its offer of pardon and newness of life it brings the very power of God to the restoring of our souls.

Even where it remains despised and rejected by the soul of man, the Cross stands majestically. It has a patience and a promise, beyond the competence of law. Its grace will never let us go, as at some point law necessarily must. If we are burdened by the length of human waywardness, as in our questions we confessed to being, we shall find in the Cross alone a commensurate enterprise of God for its redemption. It is there that all the rich wonders of revelation, of law and prophecy find their culmination and their crown. In the end, the victory of the Cross is the victory of all that it consummates or supersedes. And likewise would the hypothesis of its failure be all inclusive. For pledged in it, so the Christian believes, is the very Godness of God.

Yet, in the last resort, the question of man's being unredeemed despite the Gospel of God in Christ cannot be faced in purely discursive terms. The answer to all queries about men being saved is the summons: 'Enter ye in. . . .' The question becomes inescapably personal. All our effort after a 'frontier theology', our hope to explore kinship of meaning between the Gospel and the Quran, must terminate in the contagion of loving Christian personality. The presence of the peace of God is the common society of men in whom it dwells and reconciles and rules.

THE GOSPEL AS AUTOBIOGRAPHY

The Early Church, with apologies to Aristotle, seems to have been a very peripatetic affair. It was very much out on the highways and byways of the world. It had outstanding leaders who wrote epistles because they were inveterate travellers. It was a fellowship which proved too big for a runaway slave to elude even though he fled anonymously all the way from Colosse to Rome. And later after his discovery of personal faith it returned him the whole long distance with a most delightful commendation (the Epistle to Philemon) and a reconciled heart. It was truly well-travelled, with a positive habit of neglecting and forgetting the frontiers that normally divided peoples and cultures, classes and types. If we enter imaginatively into all that the letters of the New Testament imply we cannot doubt that, if it was the Empire which made the roads, it was the faith which made the journeys. 'Your feet shod with the readiness of the Gospel' was no remote exhortation. It was a rich and constant fact.

For the most part, it was a fellowship of very simple travellers, wayfarers of the Spirit, ordinary folk who were ready to let the significance of the Gospel be autobiographical. For it is when truth enters into biography and biography becomes the vehicle of truth that we have feet and sandals in their proper partnership. That is precisely the meaning of the metaphor. Only as sandals are worn on feet do they really come into their own. In being shod is the partnership of the presence of the peace. In hearts and minds that love and know it, the Gospel finds its local habitation, even as fire in coals and light in lamps. The Christian is the personal dimension of the Gospel.

Not in mere assertion, but by the mediation of the human presence and the personal equation, is the peace of God made known. The good news of man's remaking is proclaimed by the remade. 'Let the redeemed of the Lord say so.' For who else can or will? Men must embody, in what they are, what God has done. The living personality is the credential of the Gospel. Persons in the fellowship, of every walk and sort, are the evidential form of its validity. A meeting with people becomes sacramentally a meeting with the power and love of God. Sandals are simple and lowly enough, but all these meanings are within the homely picture they provide. It is in the lives of the people of faith that the Word of the faith walks with all its benison among men. That was how the Ephesian Christians understood their calling and how, in their jostling city with its multiplied idols and its desperate hearts, the Ephesian citizens became aware of the God of peace. There in the community of faith they could read the actuality of the peace of God since it had gathered into one before their eyes the diversities of Jew and Roman, Greek and barbarian, free-born and slave. Men who would have found it difficult understanding, or even heeding, the Epistle to the Ephesians could not fail to recognize the Gospel when it came sandalled among them in the persons of their fellow-men and threw their idol-makers into panic for their livelihood.

That human biography in which the Gospel, we may say, 'finds its feet' is, by virtue of the very nature of the Gospel, also corporate biography. The stuff of it is personal but the consensus is communal. The Church, as the corporate entity, finds its true vocation in embodying this truth. In all the foregoing little has been said about the direct enlargement of the Church, which has been seen as entirely instrumental to the business for which it exists. It is sometimes said that the job of the Church in the world is to extend itself. That is only partially true. The real fact in the New Testament needs to be carefully stated. For the suspicion that the Christian Church only relates itself to other faiths with a view to growing more numerous at their expense often proves a stubborn factor in men's disinclination to listen to its witness. They mistake the witness for a self-interested effort after religious aggrandizement.

The Church lives, let us be clear, to bear witness unto the Truth. This is its manward vocation, unmistakably implicit in the sandals' metaphor, just as its whole Godward vocation is to worship and adore the God of that truth. The ground of its address to the world is simply the wonder and the Gospel of Christ. It betrays its real nature if it thinks in quasi-national terms of its world mission, in terms, that is, akin to

141

those in which the vigorous missionary activities of Judaism were conducted in the days of the New Testament. For the making of proselytes to Judaism was a kind of spiritual imperialism in that the central announcement was an offer of naturalization into Jewry. The truth, so to speak, was a means to communal egotism and the convert was a trophy. Hence the fearful denunciation uttered by our Lord against 'their compassing sea and land' with that intent (Matt. 23.15).

It must not be so with the Church. The invitation of the Gospel does not come from a racial expression, nor does it invite into one. It begins by confessing the equality of all men both within and without it. It is not the favour of an *élite* but the debt of the forgiven; not the condescension of the superior but the hospitality of the love of God. 'All imperialisms', remarks Professor Dodd, 'are a denial of the fundamental unity of mankind'[1] and not least those that are spiritual. It is all too easy for the Church in mission in the world to fail in subduing the accidental, peripheral features of its life to its central vocation. It exists to give, not to get; to preach, not to strive; to welcome, not to proselytize.

Is it then to be totally uninterested in its numbers, its expansion, its recruits, its baptisms? Hardly. But the place of these must be always reverently subdued to its true *raison d'être* towards the world. Its significance is always and only derivative from the significance of Christ: it is to give itself that men may find Him. The true esteem of the Church is the true reputation of its Lord. It must invite men to itself as the consequence and corollary of their response to Him. It presents itself as the servant and setting of His availability to the world. It says to those who recognize the

[1] C. H. Dodd, *The Meaning of Paul for Today*, New York, Meridian Books, 1957, p. 45. The whole chapter 'The Quest of the Divine Commonwealth' illuminates the issue here.

meaning of His Gospel that the Church is the historic and actual condition of His accessibility. If men in the contemporary world find their life in Christ they cannot miss their duty to that corporate fellowship by whose ministry and fidelity they discovered Him. No man comes into a Churchless Christ. Whether he fully knows it or not, he is indebted for his saving awareness of the Saviour of the world to the Scriptures and the continuity of the living Word of faith in the fellowship of the Holy Spirit. Any man who has awakened to Christ is properly alerted to his obligation to Christ's Church. If he loves its Master, he can hardly spurn His servant. But it must always be the Church for the sake of Christ, not Christ for the sake of the Church.

'We commend not ourselves', said the apostle and surely this is what he meant. We go among men, in the power and fellowship of a community of faith which we consider to be the proper home of their souls, only because it is a home too rich and wonderful to be ours alone and because it is a home which He has constituted by being Who He is. There is, however, in our offer of its openness to all who will, nothing of a national or collective sort of self-assertion. We do not base ourselves upon any false notion of cultural ascendancy because we are within it. Its open-doored front on to humanity is simply the form of our loyalty to its meaning as the community of the loving hospitality of God. It is a fellowship of debtors, not seeking to be ministered unto – in all the subtle senses that attach to studied superiority, to dignity and even to trusts and goodnesses – but to minister.

The good news must fashion us in its own likeness. What else is it but the amazing Gospel of the self-giving God in Christ? This is the good news that relates us to the world in its own temper and after its own heart. These are the shoes: ours the feet.

143

Word-List of Islamic Terms

Though almost all the following expressions are explained and illustrated in the course of the book, it is thought that readers may find it convenient for reference to gather them into a brief glossary. In the text transliteration marks, indicating length of vowels and quality of consonants etc., are dispensed with for reasons of economy. Here they are inserted. This Word-list obviates the need for an Index. Readers will find some of these terms italicized in the text and others not. Where a word, like Sufism, seems to be already somewhat Anglicized, italics are not used. But where it is clearly technical, like *Tasliyah*, they are. A decision on such points may well be a little arbitrary. In one or two cases, like Islam and Muslim, it is useful to distinguish different meanings by using or not using italics.

Ādhān The calling, or summoning, of the faithful to prayer in Islam, from the minaret. The Englished word 'muezzin' is the name of the man who utters the call. Each of the five occasions of prayer daily is prefaced by the Ādhān. Many mosques are nowadays equipped with loud-speaker devices for this purpose. But the man on the parapet above the rooftops remains a symbol of the world of the mosque.

Anṣār The Muslim calendar begins, in the thirteenth year (or thereabouts) of the Prophet's preaching and the fifty-third or so of his age, with the Hijrah (q.v.) to Medina from Mecca. Those who welcomed Muḥammad on his arrival at the new city-centre of his movement, or who facilitated the migration by their prior assurances of allegiance, are known as 'the Helpers', or Anṣār, those by whose co-operation the greatest episode in Islam's genesis was 'made successful'. These Medinan 'aiders' also assisted in the settlement of the emigrant, Meccan co-religionaries, in goods and property (see Muhājirūn).

Āyāt A plural word (sing. Āyah) denoting a verse of the Qur'ān. The root meaning is 'a sign', each sentence of the Holy Book taking its place in the total volume which, as a whole, is the supreme miracle of God's revelation. But an Āyah is also a 'sign' in the wider sense of any action, phenomenon, or situation, in nature, in history, or in experience, through which God communicates His will. The Qur'ān is full of the theme of God's drawing the attention 'of a people who understand' to that which He has to reveal.

Bismillāh A noun formed from a phrase and denoting it; the phrase being 'In the name of God'. It opens every Surah, or chapter, of the Qur'ān except Surah ix.

Dār al-Islām ⎫ These contrasted phrases indicate 'the House-
Dār al-Ḥarb ⎭ hold of Islam' and 'the Household of non-Islam' (or lit. 'of war'). The faith of the Prophet divided humanity into one supreme division only, namely that between belief and unbelief, between surrender and obduracy. The Qur'ān is full of the distinction. It was held that the obligation resting on the former was to bring the latter into proper submission (see Jihād). Dār al-Ḥarb was so called because, being not yet amenable to the faith and empire of Islam, it was legitimately and properly the potential arena of conflict unto submission, into which it was the obligatory duty of Muslim faith and rule to penetrate. It could not expect peace (salām) with Islam until it came into Islam (surrender to God).

Dhikr The term denotes the theory and practice of sense-transcendance taught and followed by Islamic mysticism. The technique varied widely but its essence lies in the studied recollection (mention) of the name of God in rhythmic sequence and to the accompaniment, very often, of bodily movements calculated to concentrate the mind on God by prepossessing or subduing the external senses which are the occasion normally of distraction from Him.

Furqān One of the titles used of the Qur'ān in the Qur'ān and sometimes used also of the previous Scriptures, like the books of Moses or Jesus, in which Islam believes. The word means 'criterion' or 'means to discrimination', that by which

146

things are 'separated' into their proper classes. Thus the Qur'ān is that by which the Muslim knows the true from the false, the right from the wrong.

The term is also used to characterize the 'day of decision' or 'battle' of Badr, on which the Muslim forces won their first and most renowned victory over their adversaries and on which, therefore, God set His discriminatory seal of approval and validity upon them. (See Appendix of *City of Wrong*, Amsterdam, 1959, p. 224).

Ḥajj The official Great Pilgrimage to Mecca, during Dhū al-Ḥajj or the month of pilgrimage, the last month in the Muslim calendar. Pilgrimage to Mecca from the Hijaz and beyond was of long tradition prior to Islam and shorn of pagan associations was incorporated into the new faith. It remains one of the most potent 'sacraments' of Islamic history and unity. The terms Ḥājj, or Ḥājjī denote one who has accomplished the pilgrimage, which every Muslim not reasonably hindered should attempt once at least in a lifetime.

Ḥanīfs A fascinating, but still somewhat enigmatic movement towards monotheism in pre-Islamic Arabia from which Muḥammad may have drawn much inspiration and stimulus. These men anticipated his nausea over idolatry, though their own antecedents and activities are far from clear. Other figures in the far past, like Abraham, are also thought of as 'Ḥanīfs' – men of pure faith amid an idolatrous context. The presence of these men in Arabia in the century before Muḥammad must be kept in mind in estimating the Jāhiliyyah (q.v.).

Hijrah The migration of the original Islamic community from Mecca to Medina in the most formative occasion in Islamic history. The Hijrah is the hinge of what may properly be called 'the tale of two cities'. It begins 'the years of the Hijrah' and is in its own way the 'Exodus' of Islam, when the preaching became a polity and the Prophet a ruler.

Ijmā' The Islamic equivalent of *consensus fidelium* and a source of Law, complementary to the Qur'ān and Tradition. The term means the drawing together of approval into a converging acceptance. The idea rests upon the assurance that 'God's people, as such, will never agree on an error'. So in the formative days of Islamic Sharī'ah, when gaps in the revealed law still awaited categorical direction the documents did not supply, the mind of the community became the source of definition. In modern times there is in the principle of consensus a wide potential institution of *vox populi* which conservatives fear and suspect and others welcome.

Ijtihād The means to Ijmā'. Consensus does not come haphazardly. It pre-supposes competent, expert direction and initiative. Thus by Ijtihād (lit. endeavour or enterprise) qualified pundits, legists, authorities would pioneer interpretations of proper sources to meet emergent needs in law. Such initiatives shaped and made possible, but had to be confirmed by, the resultant general acceptance or Ijmā'. The range and conditions of Ijtihād are a large issue in contemporary Islam.

Islām The word, italicized, is used to distinguish the inner idea of surrender to the Divine will revealed in the Divine law, from the institutional and historical forms of the community of such surrender. The distinction may be challenged in some quarters, but it has its urgent point. For *Islām* is something that men do, which may or may not be synonymous with the Islam into which they are born and to which they traditionally belong. As in all other realms, the institutional and formal may so easily overlay, displace or even usurp the essential. (One may compare the fortunes of words like 'apostolic' and 'Apostolic', '*ecclesia*' and 'Ecclesiastical', in other quarters.)

Isnād Traditions of Muḥammad require to be attested and validated by a 'chain' of attestors who go back without break from the last reporter to the eye-witness or companion of the Prophet. Such a chain is the Isnād, or support, on which the traditions 'lean' or depend for reliability. There was a meticulous and exacting science of tradition attestation, involving subtle and painstaking research into biography and history. In general traditions were valid, not by the credibility or self-evident quality of their content, but the strength or otherwise of their formal isnād.

148

Word-List of Islamic Terms

Istighfār The act of 'seeking forgiveness' from God. The command so to do is Quranic and enters deeply into Muslim devotional life. For it is God Whom supremely our wrong-doing concerns and it is from Him that all forgiveness derives.

Iṭmi'nān A characteristic term of Muslim devotion, implying 'tranquillity', the end of that restlessness which afflicts men, as Augustine said, outside God and His peace. 'Resting in Thee' and being consequently at peace in oneself is the state of Iṭmi'nān to which Islam invites the believer and which is recognizably achieved by many a Ṣufi devotee and many a humble soul. It is the experimental corollary of the reliability of God.

Jāhiliyyah 'The Days of Ignorance' prior to the coming of Islam. It is traditional in Islamic history to emphasize the darkness prevailing in Arabia in pre-Islamic times, though the fact of the Ḥanīfs (q.v.) must mean that the darkness was not totally unrelieved. This view of the past is the obverse side of the conviction that 'the true light now shineth'.

Jihād The obligation of Muslims to exert themselves 'in the way of the Lord', for the dissemination and advancement of Islam. Since Islam did not distinguish between faith and rule, the spread of the one was axiomatically the enlargement of the other. Hence the Quranic dictum that it is better to fight than to suffer the faith to succumb. In mystical thought, the great Jihād is the inward struggle against all that is contrary to the rule of God and the discipline of surrender in the believer's heart.

Ka'bah The cube-like structure in the centre of the Great Mosque in Mecca, thought by Muslims the centre of the earth, circumambulated by pilgrims and containing the famous Black Stone. It is believed to have been erected by Abraham, the first Muslim, and it is the point of Muslim direction in prayer.

Khalīfah This word, anglicized into 'Caliph', means literally one who fills the room of, and so follows, succeeds or replaces. Historically the Caliph was the successor of Muḥammad as ruler and the Caliphate as an institution came in

149

theory to be a *sine qua non* of Islam. But this political institution, nevertheless, has no Quranic ground. There the Khalīfah once referred to (the only other occurrence relating to David) is man himself, Adam, the representative prototype of mankind. He is described as set in the earth to be God's viceregent or representative having dominion over things on God's behalf. Sometimes Muslim prayer reverently reverses the role and a man on pilgrimage may ask God to take his place as head over his house and watch over his family until his return.

Khaṭīb The mosque preacher, whose function is to deliver the Khuṭbah or formal sermon at the Friday congregational prayer.

Miḥrāb The niche in the mosque wall which indicates the direction of the Ka'bah at Mecca (q.v.). It is generally semi-circular with fluted roof and decorated with calligraphic inscriptions. The Imām, in leading the prayers, stands before it.

Minbar The mosque pulpit, usually in the form of receding steps set at right angles to the mosque wall, on the right side (worshipper's view) of the miḥrāb. Surmounted with an ornate lintel at the foot and leading to a raised platform above, the Minbar is occupied only by the Khaṭīb. So it is a sort of *cathedra* or place of authoritative declaration of allegiance and its meaning in Islam.

Muhājirūn The plural noun (nominative) denoting those who made the Hijrah, the Meccan Muslims who journeyed to Medina and with the help of the Anṣār (q.v.) became founder members of the new Medinan, Islamic polity.

Mujtahid The 'doer' of Ijtihād (q.v.). The qualifications pre-requisite to Ijtihād were traditionally very exacting and strenuous, and included expert knowledge of Arabic grammar, exegesis, history, the law and fiqh or juris-prudence. In Shī'ah Islam the mujtahid had a still more exalted role. In modern times, with the demand for the re-opening of the 'door' or occasion of Ijtihād, there has been a growing plea for the laicization of the qualifications required in mujtahids, so that initiative in public opinion within and behind law can be exercised by Muslims of status in the ordinary community, without the minutiae of the old stringent patterns.

Mushrik He who commits Shirk (q.v.): the antithesis of the Muslim, the idolater, who erects false absolutes and deifies them, so defying the sole sovereignty of God and alienating His indivisible rule. In Muḥammad's days the Quraish people were the arch-Mushrikūn. Who are they today?

Muslim He who does 'islām' (q.v.), the one who confesses the Shahādah (q.v.) and recognizes the articles of faith and fulfils the duties of religion. Within this communal and familiar definition is the further and more ultimate sense of the muslim, as one who is adequately cognizant, in mind, heart and will, of the Godness of God. There is much internal debate in Islam today about who is the Muslim and therein much questioning by some Muslims of the muslim status of other Muslims. In some usages the adjective 'Islamic' is reserved for the ideal that ought to be, while 'Muslim' describes what actually is.

Niyyah A basic concept in Islam: the Five Pillars of Religion, witness, prayer, almsgiving, fasting and pilgrimage, must all be prefaced by the declaration of 'intention', or Niyyah. Acts of devotion must be deliberate and conscious. That is not truly done which is not truly intended.

Qiblah The direction of prayer, marked by the miḥrāb (q.v.), towards the Ka'bah in Mecca. Muslim prayer was originally toward Jerusalem but shortly after the Hijrah was changed to Mecca. In Surah ii, the Qur'ān insists that this means no localization of God, but the change was at the outset 'a hard thing' for those who had been nurtured in the monotheist faith of which Jerusalem was the age-long type, and in the folly of idolatry with which Mecca was still full. But the change must be regarded as prospective of Mecca's ultimate conquest and cleansing. The Qiblah is the great 'sacrament' of unity for Muslims.

Qur'ān The name of the Islamic Holy Book, meaning the 'recital' or utterance of that which is inscribed. It derives from the command of Surah xcvi: 'Recite in the name of thy Lord', belonging, in all likelihood, to Muḥammad's inaugural vision. The word Qur'ān may relate to the eternal Book in Heaven; that Book in its Tanzīl or descent to, into and upon the mind and tongue of the Prophet; the subsequent utterance of it in his preaching; its recording on earth and its recital on the lips of readers and all the faithful. The word involves the twin ideas of the givenness of what is written and the expressedness of what is uttered.

Al-Raḥmān al-Raḥīm A couplet of Divine names always linked with the Bismillāh (q.v.). The root R Ḥ M means 'mercy' and the derivatives here indicate the mercy that is God's as a property (irrespective of particular occasions of its exercise) and that mercy in particular operation and direction. Though 'the compassionate, the merciful' is the usual translation, 'the merciful Lord of mercy' draws closer to the precise sense.

Rak'ah (pl.: Raka'āt) The term denoting the sequence of movements which make up a complete act of prayer, two, three or four of which may be required to fulfil the Ṣalāt (q.v.) according to the time of day. The movements pass through erect posture, to squatting, prostrating, repeated to the erect stance and the greeting after the final Rak'ah.

Ramaḍān The name of the pre-Islamic month with which fasting was connected, it passed to the obligatory Muslim fast of twenty-eight days from sunrise to sunset daily. The fast implies no asceticism for its own sake but yearly proclaims the ascendancy of the soul, the discipline of the body and the duty of gratitude for the good things of life. It is also a time of intensified devotion.

Ṣalāt The act of Muslim prayer, the 'doing' of which, as the reiterated Quranic phrase expresses it, is a prime condition of a valid Islam. It is incumbent five times daily, when the Ādhān calls, is preceded by ablution and conforms to careful patterns of bodily movements and recited words of praise and ascription. The only element of petition is that found in the plea of the Fātiḥah, or opening Surah of the Qur'ān, which is recited: 'Guide us in the straight path. . . .'

Shahādah The first of the Pillars of Religion, the confession that 'There is no god save God and Muḥammad is the apostle (or messenger) of God'.

Word-List of Islamic Terms

Sharī'ah The term that denotes the sacred law of Islam. Root meaning has to do with 'the way of what is right'. Its sources are the Qur'ān and Tradition, complemented by Qiyās (or analogy) and Ijtihād. Though necessarily incorporating large areas of customary law, the underlying concept of the Sharī'ah is that law is Divinely willed and enjoined. Its validity arises, not from pragmatic, rational or habitual grounds, but from the Divine decree. Of late there have been wide divergencies from Shar'ī law, even in what has to do with personal status – the area always least amenable to change. But something of the old concept of a state and a jurisprudence which are what they are for the basic reason that so God has ordained remains under the new codes and cases.

Shirk The Muslim anathema against idols is a basic concept throughout Islam and in this book's attempt to interpret the Muslim. The crude translation 'association' invites many wrong notions. Shirk is that which Islam vetoes with utmost abhorrence – the act of attributing to other than God the power, right, worship, knowledge, sovereignty, which properly belong to God alone.

Sufism This word, with anglicized termination, derives from Sūfī, meaning 'mystic' (the most likely origin takes us to Sūf, wool, the wearing of which, as opposed to silks and satins, marked the simplicity and ascetic discipline within which Sufism was generated). The whole movement extended widely and ramified diversely, at times carrying forward in history the major forms of Islamic virility and fervour.

Sujūd The prostration in the Rak'ah, which brings man's brow down to the earth, below the prayer mat (or pebble) on which the worshipper lays his forehead in the act of reverence. The onlooker finds the corporate Sujūd of long serried rows of pray-ers the most impressive symbol of Islam.

Tafsīr The exegesis of the Qur'ān. The greatest exegetes like Al-Baidawi and Al-Zamakhshari set a tradition of close textual study based on grammar and illustration from the body of Ḥadīth or prophetic precedent. The pattern of

153

Quranic exegesis is a growing issue and a large question in contemporary Islam.

Takbīr The saying of Allāhu Akbar, or 'God is most great'. In the Arabic phrase a comparative form is used for which no comparison is feasible. Hence the sense becomes an overwhelming superlative.

Taqwā The devout and trustful piety, or sense of Divine providence and splendour, with man's finitude, frailty and creaturehood, which constitutes perhaps the most characteristic moral qualities of practising Muslims.

Ta'wīdh The act of 'seeking refuge with God', derived from the verb used in the last two Surahs of the Qur'ān. 'I seek refuge with God' from evil, from temptation, from the menace of the world unseen and the wiles of the tempter.

Tauḥīd The positive antithesis of Shirk (q.v.), the loyal recognition and assertion of the Unity of God, both propositionally as a belief and actually as an attitude.

'Ulamā' A plural noun describing the learned in Muslim law and theology, who have achieved this rank in houses of learning like Al-Azhar in Cairo or the Qairawīn in Fez.

Wudū' The act of ablution according to ritual requirements, which precedes the Ṣalāt.

Zakāt The obligation of every Muslim to bring alms for use 'in the cause (lit. in the way) of God'. This comprehensive phrase covers a wide variety of purposes relating to the sustaining inwardly of the Muslim community and its propagation outwardly. By the proportion of one's income that is given (variable according to the type and source of the property or income) one 'cleanses' or legitimizes what one retains. Zakāt is thus the condition, in Islamic economic theory, of the validity of private property. Its essential meaning is that there is a public stake in all private ownership which must be acknowledged.

Short Book-List

The two introductory books mentioned on p. 27 give a general synopsis of Islam and have useful classified bibliographies. Extensive bibliography will also be found in the author's *The Call of the Minaret*, New York, Oxford University Press, 1956, pp. 359–367. Readers are referred to these sources. What follows is in no sense a reading-list in Islamics but simply a brief selection of certain titles, with comments in some cases, illustrating the themes of Part I, and Parts 2 and 3.

A. PART 1

Abdul Latif, Syed, *Towards a Re-Orientation of Islamic Thought*, Hyderabad, 1954.

An Indian Muslim venture in corporate thought about contemporary obligations of Islam and Muslims.

Ali, Abdallah Yusuf, *The Holy Quran*, 2 vols., Lahore, 1937–1938.

An interpretative translation by a prominent leader of exegesis and thought.

Ali, Muhammad, *The Living Thoughts of the Prophet Muhammad*, London, Cassell, 1947.

One of the ablest and most prolific writers of the Lahore section of the Ahmadiyyah Movements presents the Prophet for the non-Muslim.

Arberry, A. J., *The Koran Interpreted*, 2 vols., London, Allen and Unwin, 1955.

A well-known Western orientalist translates the Quran with a skilful eye for the original cadence and rhythm. It is this which the title has in mind and not, as might naturally be supposed, any attempt at commentary.

Asad, Muhammad, *Road to Mecca*, New York, Scribners, 1955.
A former Viennese journalist and traveller narrates in eloquent prose the story of his personal journey into Islam.

Bennabi, Malek, *Vocation de l'Islam*, Paris, 1954.
Meditations on twentieth-century Muslim meanings by an Algerian man of letters.

Brohi, A. K., *Adventure in Self-Expression*, Karachi, Din Muhammadi Press, 1955.

An interesting document of personal reflection on Islam today by a lawyer who took part in the drafting of the Basic Principles Resolution during constitutional debates in Pakistan.

Donaldson, Dwight M., *Studies in Muslim Ethics*, London, SPCK, 1953.

Fisher, Sidney M., editor, *Social Forces in the Middle East*, Ithaca, Cornell University Press, 1955.

One of the more penetrating collections of papers and articles on the area which appear with great frequency from conferences and colloquia.

Frye, Richard N., editor, *Islam and the West*, Gravenhage, Mouton and Co., 1957.

Another of the above, being lectures at the Harvard Summer School on 'Islamic Renaissance – Egypt, Turkey and Pakistan'. Of special value is the paper by Howard A. Reed, 'The Religious Life of Modern Turkish Muslims'.

Gibb, H. A. R., *Modern Trends in Islam*, Chicago, 1947.

A skilful, expert analysis of contemporary Islam which must be used, however, in the light of the decade that has elapsed since its appearance.

Hazard, H. W. and Cook, H. L., *Atlas of Islamic History*, 3rd edition, Princeton University Press, 1954.

Levy, Reuben, *Structure of Islam*, London, Cambridge University Press, 1956.

A revision of the author's well-known *Introduction to the Sociology of Islam*, 2 vols., London, 1931–1933. A most useful compendium of studies on Islamic life and institutions.

Short Book-List

Morrison, S. A., *Middle East Survey*, London, SCM Press, 1954.

One of the best of the short, single-author analyses of contemporary issues, political, social and religious.

Roolvink, R., *Historical Atlas of the Islamic Peoples*, Amsterdam, Djambatan, 1957.

Schroeder, Eric, *Muhammad's People*, Portland, Maine, U.S.A.

A fascinating and comprehensive presentation of the history and 'genius' of Islam through a wise anthology of Muslim writing.

Smith, Wilfred Cantwell, *Islam in Modern History*, Princeton University Press, 1957.

This work is an example, to quote its own objective, of 'the capacity to construct religious statements that will be intelligible and cogent in two different religious traditions simultaneously'. It sets out a careful and imaginative analysis of the stresses and potentialities of Islam. The author is Director of the Institute of Islamic Studies, of McGill University, Montreal, Canada.

Tritton, A. S., *Islam*, London, Hutchinson, 1951.

A useful and erudite compendium in a somewhat laconic and unimaginative style.

Watt, W. Montgomery, *Muhammad at Mecca*, London, Oxford University Press, 1952.

Watt, W. Montgomery, *Muhammad at Medina*, London, Oxford University Press, 1955.

Biographies of the Prophet have been in full tide in this century in the Muslim world. Among those originating in Western scholarship these twin volumes, which utilize the familiar division in Muhammad's story, represent perhaps the most interesting of biographical ventures in English. The author draws with meticulous care upon contemporary sources and one of his main objectives is to identify the economic factors underlying the rise of Islam in so far as these may be discernible in the social and tribal character of its early adherents.

B. PARTS 2 AND 3

Abdul Hakim, Khalifah, *Islamic Ideology*, Lahore, 1954.

An interesting compendium of twentieth-century thought and reaction within Pakistani Islam on a variety of topics, philosophical and sociological.

Ashby, Philip H., *The Conflict of Religions*, New York, 1955.

Baly, Denis, *Multitudes in the Valley*, Greenwich, Connecticut, Seabury Press, 1957.

Bennabi, Malek, *Lebbeik, Pèlerinage des Pauvres*, Algiers, 1948.

A reflective novel by one of the most articulate of North African Muslim writers, in which a depraved 'rake' finds a new life through a personal crisis of pilgrimage to Mecca.

Bousquet, Georges H., *La Morale de l'Islam et son Ethique Sexuelle*, Paris, A. Maisonneuve, 1953.

A useful study of the concept of sex in Islam: a straightforward exposition of a theme where there is actually much alienation and potentially much common need between religions.

Dillistone, Frederick W., *Christianity and Symbolism*, London, Collins, 1955.

Dillistone, Frederick W., *Christianity and Communication*, London, Collins, 1956.

Gardet, Louis and Anawati, C. G., *Introduction à la Théologie Musulmane*, Paris, 1948.

Jurji, Edward J., *The Christian Interpretation of Religion*, New York, Macmillan, 1952.

Hocking, William E., *Living Religions and a World-Faith*, New York, Scribners, 1940.

Hussein, Muhammad Kamel, *City of Wrong*, Cairo, 1954, Translated from the Arabic, 1959, and published by Djambatan, Amsterdam, with the sub-title: *A Friday in Jerusalem*, with Introduction by the translator.

A sensitive and perceptive study of 'the sin of world' as a Muslim author finds it in the Good Friday narrative. A most fruitful work of inter-religious thought, from within Islam.

158

Short Book-List

Jones, L. Bevan, *Christianity Explained to Muslims*, Calcutta, YMCA Press, 1938.

A useful manual of some of the main issues lying between Christian faith and Muslim doctrine, with careful documentation and special reference to the contra-Christian publications of the Ahmadiyah Movements.

Kraemer, Hendrick, *The Christian Message in a non-Christian World*, London, Edinburgh House Press, 1938.

Kraemer, Hendrick, *Religion and the Christian Faith*, London, Lutterworth Press, 1956.

Two monumental works from a well-loved, if always erudite and sometimes exasperating authority.

Operation Reach, Jerusalem, 1957–1959.

A series of Study Papers, prepared under the Near East Christian Council's Study fellowship and setting out a sequence of Islamic themes. Obtainable from the Council's offices, P.O. Box 235, Beirut, Lebanon.

Padwick, Constance E., *Call to Istanbul*, London, Longmans, Green, 1958.

An intimate study of a Christian's life-investment in the spiritual service of Turkey and the Turks.

Padwick, Constance E., *Temple Gairdner of Cairo*, London, SPCK, 1928.

Perhaps the most moving study of Muslim-Christian interrelations in biographical form.

Padwick, Constance E., *With Him in His Temptations*, London, SPCK, 1949.

A study of discipleship in the trust of Christ illuminated by reflections on the Temptations besetting Him in the wilderness and related to the criticism of features of the Gospels made by Muslim writers of our time.

Padwick, Constance E., *Common Words of Muslim Prayer*, London, SPCK, 1959.

Distilling a lifetime's work and devotion, this book presents and examines the vocabulary, attitudes and spirit of Muslim Prayer manuals used through the variety of Sufi or mystical orders and fraternities. A mine of information and a gate of access for the imaginative.

Shah, Sirdar Iqbal Ali, *Lights of Asia*, London, 1934.

A prolific Muslim writer offers an interpretation of great religions in his own words but as if from within each. The section on Christianity is deep and sensitive.

J. Windrow Sweetman, *Islam and Christian Theology*, Part I, Vols. 1 and 2, Part II, Vol. 1, London, Lutterworth Press, 1945–1955.

Voillaume, R., *Seeds of the Desert; The Legacy of Charles de Foucauld*, London, Burns, Oates, 1955.

A Classic of devotion and travail in self-disappropriation and the expression of Christ.